Practical
Fishing Knots

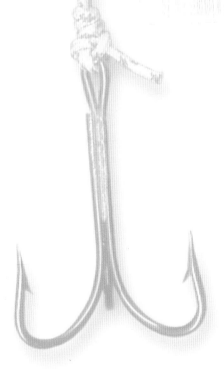

D0922460

A competent angler named Pook
Said: "I learned all my knots from a book.
Now, by tying them right,
My lines remain tight
And I land all the fish that I hook."

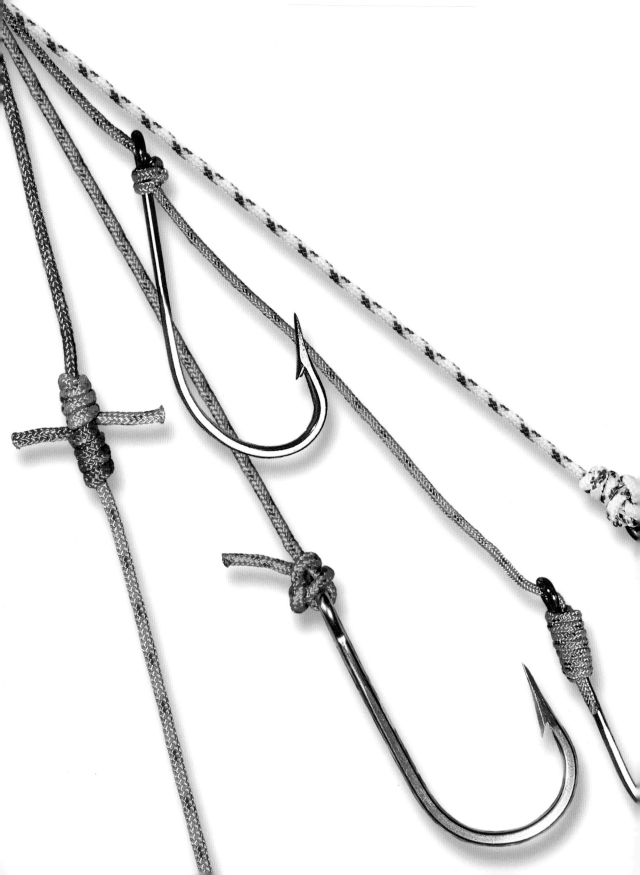

Practical
Fishing Knots

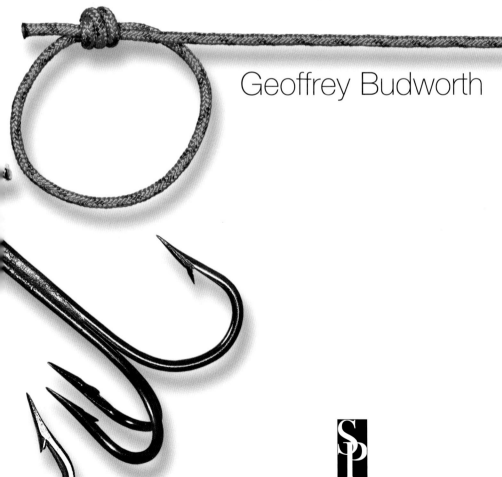

Geoffrey Budworth

Skyhorse Publishing

Skyhorse Publishing books may be purchased in bulk at special discounts for sales promotion, corporate gifts, fund-raising, or educational purposes. Special editions can also be created to specifications. For details, contact the Special Sales Department, Skyhorse Publishing, 555 Eighth Avenue, Suite 903, New York, NY 10018 or info@skyhorsepublishing.com.

www.skyhorsepublishing.com

10 9 8 7 6 5 4 3 2 1

Library of Congress Cataloging-in-Publication Data

Budworth, Geoffrey.
  Practical fishing knots / Geoffrey Budworth.
     p. cm.
  Includes index.
  ISBN 978-1-60239-993-8 (pbk. : alk. paper)
  1. Fishing knots. I. Title.
  SH452.9.K6B844 2010
  799.12--dc22
                              2009047921

Printed in China

Picture acknowledgments

Archivo Iconografico, S.A./CORBIS: 13; Bettman/CORBIS: 12; Kevin R. Flemming/CORBIS: 74–75; David T. Greenwood/CORBIS: 56–57; Layne Kennedy/CORBIS: 22–23; Kevin R. Morris/CORBIS: 14; William Sallaz/CORBIS: 2–3; Kirsten Soderlind/CORBIS: 132–133; Dale C. Spartas/CORBIS: 10–11, 100–101.

Contents

Introduction

Learn just one knot, use it often, and the cost of this book will be amply repaid. Acquire several and the time spent with rod, lines, and tackle will be enriched. For knots are the one item of gear that anglers must fabricate themselves; and, as they will always be the weakest link in any rig, their selection and tying must aim to reduce the problem.

It pays, in terms of tackle safeguarded, bait and fish caught, to know what to use, when and how and why. And, unlike other gear bought at some cost from one's favorite fishing emporium, knots can be had for no more outlay than the time and effort taken to learn how to tie them, and then employ them. They occupy no space in a tackle box and add no weight to it, and you will not be compelled, in an age of heightened security at airports, to stow them in the airplane's hold. Knowledge of knots is retained in the mind and fingers. They can safely be carried into the passenger cabin where, to combat fear or boredom, you can gain practice at tying them during the flight.

I am indebted to Paul Honess, marketing coordinator for Marlow Ropes Limited of Hailsham, England—the leading manufacturer of yacht ropes—for generously supplying the material used to illustrate most of the knots in the following pages of this book. For real fishing lines are too insubstantial for the portrayal of fishing knots, let alone to

teach their step-by-step tying methods. Similarly, hands-on learning of unfamiliar knots is best done with thicker stuff that is more forgiving to fingers that are still learning. For these reasons, all of the knots in this book are pictured in cordage that has a diameter five to ten times larger than actual mono or braided lines and leaders. Tag ends emerging from knots are also longer than they would be when tied in actual fising lines. Only when the shape and subtleties of an individual knot have become familiar should they be attempted (scaled down) using real line and, even then, this fiddly task should be tried for the first time under optimal conditions indoors, before it is performed afloat or at the waterside.

It is not easy to learn knots from a book, but it must be done from time to time because an approachable tutor may not always be available. Indeed it can be instructive to look at more than one, since authors sometimes differ in their advice and guidance, preferences, and prejudices.

The difficulty of portraying knots in two dimensions on the page restricts the choice of basic tying action described. Other more fluent, almost sleight-of-hand manipulations may ultimately be preferable, but these can only be acquired from personal coaching by experienced fishing friends, who can also suggest how the knots might be incorporated into all sorts of tackle systems or rigs.

A Knotting History

Cave dwellers surely tied knots, and there is archaeological evidence of Stone Age humankind 10,000 years ago fishing with knotted nets, as well as hand lines of gut or sinew attached to bone fish hooks. Fishing was one of the earliest practical applications of knot tying.

More than a thousand years before the birth of Christ, the ancient Greeks of Mycenae used barbed and eyed hooks of bronze . . . and they may have invented fly fishing. The Greek writer Plutarch (c.AD 46–120) believed and taught that the best fishing lines were made from the tails of thoroughbred white stallions, his reasoning—wrong, as it turned out—being that mares weakened their tail hairs with frequent splashes of urine. In fact, coarse-bred stallions, mares, and geldings all have tougher tails.

Angling enjoyed a growth spurt in Britain during the 15th to 17th centuries, before spreading as a consequence of emigration, trade, military excursions, and the writings of luminaries

Isaak Walton (1593–1683), pictured left on a fishing excursion from an engraving of 1832, was an author whose works helped to spread interest in angling.

Detail of a relief from the mastaba of the Princess Idout, Saqqara, Egypt, c.2500 BC, showing a scene of men fishing with hooks.

like Gervase Markham, Isaak Walton, Robert Venables, and Robert Nobbes, to Europe and Australia, America, and Canada. Women also made their mark. Cleopatra, the Egyptian queen from 51 to 48 BC was, it seems, an accomplished angler. The Japanese empress Zinga (AD 170–269) was cited as a model of frugality for catching a trout on a bent pin, baited with grains of rice, on a line made from threads pulled from her garment. And the legendary Dame Juliana, prioress of Sopwell (if she truly existed), was an expert with rod and line. It is recorded that she made her own horsehair lines—one hair for minnows, two for roach, and fifteen for salmon—tying them with water (or duchy) knots and binding each knot with fine silk thread. She also dyed the lines: green to mimic the water weeds in summer, yellow or brown for autumnal shades, tawny in winter and early spring.

Fly fishing in Gallatin National Forest, Montana.

Fishing lines, old and new

By the 19th century, the horsehair fishing lines that would have been familiar to Plutarch and Dame Juliana had been augmented by other natural materials such as cotton, flax, jute, gut (obtained from several creatures), and heavily oiled or greased silk. But all of them had shortcomings. Subjected to abrasion, they frayed. Weak, particularly when wet, they broke. They had to be dried meticulously after use, yet were still prone to mildew and rot, prey to insects and vermin.

Artificial filaments were discovered in the 1930s and adopted by many anglers during World War II when hostilities reduced the availability of previously imported materials. With considerably greater strength-to-weight ratios than natural materials, the new lines were lighter and thinner, so more could be wound onto a reel. By the year 2000, synthetic fishing lines were a quantum leap away from those of a century earlier.

Today's monofilaments and braids are

mere hundredths of an inch (tenths of a millimeter) in diameter, with breaking strengths that range from a mere 8 oz (0.2 kg) to 120 lbs (54 kgs) and more. The discriminating angler can obtain lines that float or sink as required, and tapered casts or leaders with graduated breaking strengths.

The two "Ps"—polyamide (nylon) and polyester (terylene, dacron)—predominate. Nylon is the stronger of the two, but loses 10% of its strength when wet, only to regain it when dry again. Terylene is 25% weaker but equally strong wet or dry. Both have melting points around 500°F (260°C) but are irremediably weakened at a much lower temperature, so they should be kept away from campfires and camping stoves. For the same reason, knotted tag ends must not be trimmed with a glowing cigarette end or the flame from a lighter.

Nylon has great natural shock-absorbing elasticity and will stretch under a load by up to 30%, returning more or less to its original length when that load is removed. Nylon mono (especially with the aid of a multiplier), while it is subject to the strain of a heavy fish and the spooled line, will be abnormally tight. Transfer it to another spool as soon as possible to allow a return to its normal state. Terylene by contrast has only a sixth of nylon's inherent elasticity, most of which may be removed during the manufacturing process.

Both nylon and terylene have a specific gravity greater than water and so will sink. They may be put away wet. Each resists attack by oils and organic solvents, as well as degradation by the ultraviolet rays in sunlight. Nylon also withstands alkalis but is vulnerable to acid, whereas terylene resists acids (but alkalis to a lesser extent). They are both very durable but deteriorate with time, even if unused, and must eventually be replaced.

The very latest high-tech development in miracle lines has made available several brands of super-lines and super-braids, stronger (strand for strand) than stainless steel, whose other properties are still being tested and evaluated.

Post-war anglers, as they became familiar with synthetics, soon discovered that previously tried-and-trusted knots were unreliable in artificial monofilaments and braids. The effectiveness of some knots was halved; others failed altogether. The immediate response was to add more twists and tucks, resulting in some inelegant and unlovely conglomerations; but, gradually, a fresh generation of fishing knots evolved.

Mid-20th-century fishing manuals featured no more than ten knots deemed vital to cope with an angling reader's needs. Today's publications pick 'n' mix from one hundred knots. Then again, taking into account an apparently unending number of variations and modifications, there are now perhaps one thousand ways of tying a fishing line.

Knot Names

The spread of angling throughout the English-speaking world led to a mind-muddling proliferation of knot names. Some archaic names have been overlaid by contemporary ones. Where form yields to function (e.g., a cat's paw becoming the offshore swivel knot) it makes sense. When whimsy is indulged in, it makes less. For example, the double fisherman's knot is a grinner, and the triple fisherman's knot (by some curious arithmetic) is a double grinner. Naming a knot after a person or place (for example the Homer Rhodes knot) adds an extra fog factor.

In still other instances, confusion reigns. The terms blood knot, nail knot, and snell knot, often prefaced by some adjective or other (quick, improved, emergency) are used, misused, and abused. Indeed, some people assert, the ubiquitous clutch of "uni" (universal) knots (*see page 18*) are just badly tied and tightened blood knots.

There is a convention that permits a knot tied by a different method for another purpose to have another name. More than one joining knot appears in several guises as a mono-to-mono, mono-to-braid, or leader-to-wire knot. The uni knot, it can be argued, falls into this category.

Finally, national and regional knot names differ so much that it can be impossible to take a knot from one publication and look it up in the index of another. The only faint hope for the eventual establishment of a common terminology may be found in people's increasing commitment to electronic communication via the Internet.

Terms and techniques

In order for knot tying instructions to make sense, some essential terms need explanation (*see illustration, below*). The end of a line or leader that is actively involved in the tying process is called the **working**

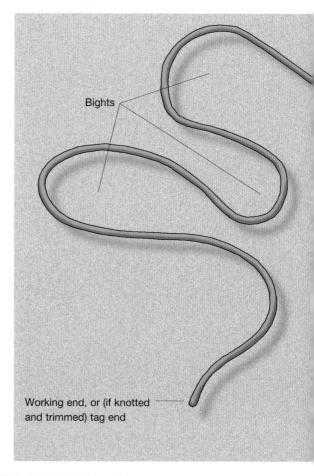

Bights

Working end, or (if knotted and trimmed) tag end

end. The other end is the **standing end**. Any inactive length of line between the two is the **standing part**. When the working end has been knotted, then what emerges from the knot (and is usually trimmed off short) becomes the **tag end**. Doubling the working end by bending it over creates a tonguelike **bight**, and this term also refers to any U-shaped section in the standing part of the line.

Once a bight acquires a **crossing point**, it becomes a **loop**, and a couple of crossing points close together make **elbows**. Knotted loops may be **fixed** or **sliding** (that is, adjustable). Sliding loops are sometimes called *nooses*.

Many angling knots depend on the friction and constriction generated by a series of wrapping turns. These knots are collectively known as **blood knots**, perhaps because their inclusion in the lashes of an 18th-century Royal Navy cat-o'-nine-tails drew blood from the backs of seamen unlucky enough to be thrashed with them. Understanding how blood knots are made is crucial to tying a number of useful angling knots.

First tie a simple overhand knot, then tuck the working end two or more times (*figure 1*). Now gently pull standing and

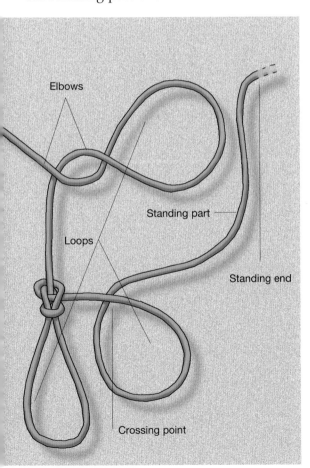

Elbows

Standing part

Loops

Standing end

Crossing point

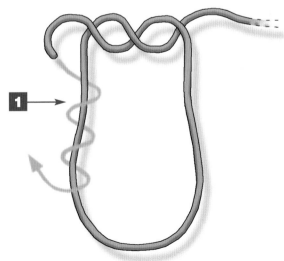

1 →

The basic blood knot

Direction
of torsion

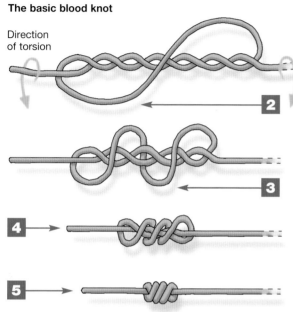

working ends in opposite directions and feel how the two entwined parts tend to unwind in the process wrapping the large loop around the knot. Encourage this by twiddling the fingers of each hand in opposite directions as illustrated (*figures 2–3*). When this latent torsion has been allowed to impose itself on the final knot form, tug the knot snug and tight (*figures 4–5*).

Once this process is mastered, blood knots can be indirectly created from a series of turns made around the standing part of the line and then **flyped** (that is, turned inside out, much like peeling off a glove or sock) into the familiar blood knot configuration. Flyping (rhymes with "typing") is a word first floated as a

knotting term in the late-19th century by the Scottish physicist Peter Guthrie Tait (1831–1901), and it resurfaced in the mid-1980s as a handy expression for a knot-tying phenomenon that is otherwise hard to explain.

For example, pass the working end of a fishing line through the eye of a hook and then twist it four or more times around its own standing part, before tucking the tag end back through the loop alongside the eye (*figure 6*). Pull firmly on the standing part, and the entwined line parts will start to unwind, at the same time wrapping the loop around in a spiral (*figure 7*). Continue to pull, and what began as a long and loose tangle will metamorphose into a compact half-blood knot (*figure 8*). This is flyping in action.

Failure to understand how blood knots are achieved directly or indirectly, as well as careless or impatient tightening, will put too much tension upon the standing part of the line (*figure 9*) and result in a distorted form of the knot (*figure 10*). Such knots occur frequently. Indeed they are portrayed in many fishing-knot manuals, although whether this is deliberate or due to misunderstanding on the part of illustrators is unclear. Anglers are divided. Some believe them to be a separate category of knot entirely and label them "uni" knots. The trouble is that uni knots are less secure than their blood knot equivalents. Also, the overriding diagonal

Flyping

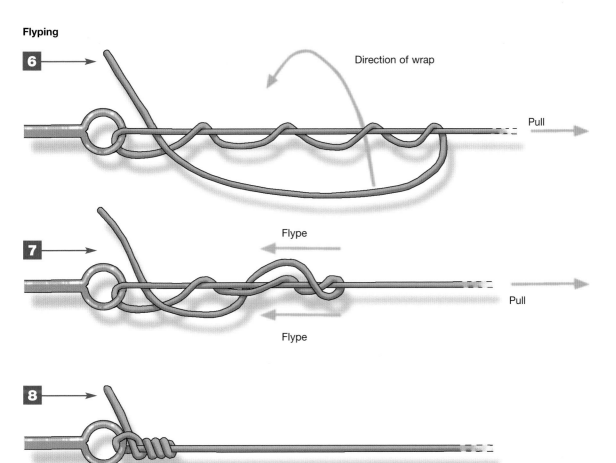

Direction of wrap

6

Pull

7

Flype

Pull

Flype

8

Distorted blood knot

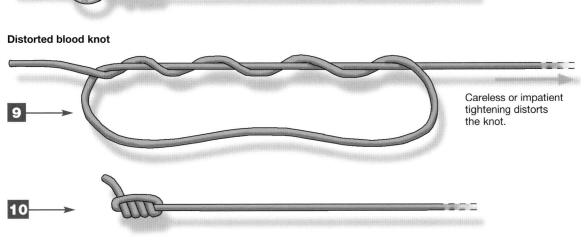

9

Careless or impatient tightening distorts the knot.

10

knot part is prone to snag, vulnerable to abrasion, and, if severed, the knot will instantly unravel. True blood knots are preferable, although it requires experience, dexterity, and some luck to achieve them. If at first you don't succeed, tie, tie, and tie again.

Most knots weaken the line in which they are tied. Worst case scenario: a simple overhand knot unintentionally acquired in line will, if overlooked and allowed to tighten, reduce the breaking strength of that line to less than half that calculated by the manufacturer for the original unknotted line. In other words the knot's strength is less than 50%. The knots selected for inclusion in this book are, when tied properly and tightened with care, all very much stronger than that. A few, such as the Bimini twist, are said to be 100% efficient (as strong as the unknotted line); but, when several different knots are used to assemble a tackle rig, what results will only be as strong as the weakest knot. Strength in a knot is its ability to withstand a load without breaking the line.

Security is a separate quality from strength but equally desirable in a fishing knot. Secure knots withstand shock loading, intermittent jerking, and a steady load without slipping or coming adrift (as opposed to breaking the line). The best of all angling knots are both strong and secure; but, as the friction and nip needed to create such paragons are achieved only by lots of twists, turns, and tucks, economic knot tying is often a compromise. Arbor knots, for instance, ought not to be subjected to heavy loading since the final few turns of line around a reel are rarely ever unwound in action. Less bulky, weaker knots are therefore allowed for this purpose.

Knot-tying tips

Tying fishing knots demands dexterous fingers, a deft touch, and keen eyesight (natural or corrected), a combination of gifts not possessed by many mortals; especially one who is cold, wet, and maybe disheartened beside the water or afloat on it in poor visibility and driving rain. Nonetheless, there is an element of craftsmanship required to tie, shape, trim, and reinforce some fishing knots. Whenever possible, this is best achieved indoors. But wherever it is done, bear in mind the following guidelines:

- A visibly damaged section of line should be discarded, or its failure may later be blamed—wrongly—on the knot.

- Knots must be accurately tied. No approximation is allowed. If even one tuck or turn goes awry, the knot is wrong.

- Wrapping turns must lie snug and tight once tightened. A bird's nest of unwanted loops and overlays will drastically weaken the knot in use. Cut it off and try again.

- The number of wrapping turns should vary with the diameter of the line in which a knot is tied: 3 or 4 turns in heavy lines tested at 50 to 100 lbs (23–45 kgs); 4 or 5 in lines of 20 to 30 lbs (9–14 kgs); 5 or 6 in lines of 12 to 18 lbs (5–8 kgs); and 6 or 7 in lines up to 10 lbs (5 kgs).

- The tension in any knot must be evenly distributed during the tying process.

- The tighter, the better, as a general rule. Knots start to slip, internal turns and tucks generate heat by friction and slice into one another, just before they break. The less slippage possible, in theory and practice, the stronger the knot.

- Lubricate complex knots prior to tightening them. Many liquids, oils, or powders will do the trick, whether a proprietary brand of some sort, or merely water, provided it is not deleterious to the line (as the digestive chemistry of saliva may be).

- Fishing knots must be shaped, slack eliminated, and tension applied, with care and patience. At the same time, unwanted crossovers must be removed. Only when the final form is inevitable may one or two sharp tugs be applied.

- Be prepared to protect fingers from cuts, when tightening heavy mono, by means of a rag or glove. Thicker lines that cannot be tightened by hand must be pulled by means of a pair of pliers.

- Trim tag ends but leave sufficient amount projecting from the knot for slippage to occur when fish are hooked. This amount could be as little as $1/16$ of an inch (0.16 cm) for light lines to $1/4$ inch (0.6 cm) for heavy ones.

- Completed knots may be rendered even more secure by a coating of nail polish, rubber-based cement, or super-glue, and further streamlined with plastic sleeves or a seizing of dental floss.

Keep these tips in mind while tightening and trimming the following knots.

"I found out that the Bimini twist is not a native dance and that you don't need an MD to tie a surgeon's knot."

—Bill Cullerton, *leading outdoorsman and producer of angling films*

Knots for Arbors, Connectors, Hooks, and Lures

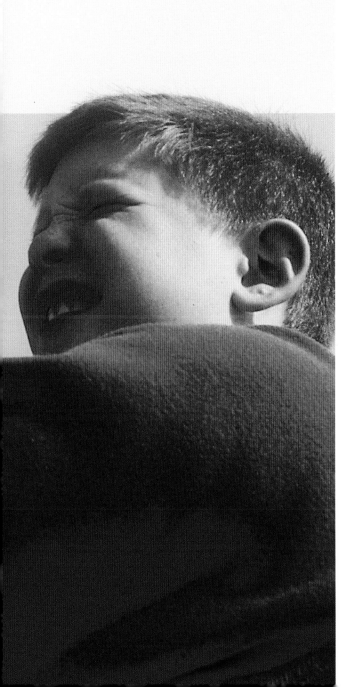

"The difference between hooking and landing fish almost solely depends on a properly tied fishing knot."

(Harry Nilsson—*The Little Red Fishing Knot Book*, 1997)

Looking to hook a big one at the Fishing Hall of Fame, Hayward, Wisconsin, 1987.

Arbor knot—method 1
(double overhand)

Function

A knot used to attach fishing line to reel, spool, or arbor need be of only moderate strength and security, as the final few turns of any backing line are seldom unwound and so the knot is rarely if ever tested by a hooked fish.

Tying

Take a turn or two around the spool or arbor and tie a double or triple blood knot (*see introduction, pages 17–18*) around the standing part of the line (*figure 1*). Tighten this knot and slide it snugly onto the spool or arbor (*figure 2*).

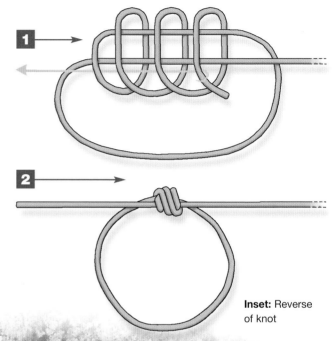

Inset: Reverse of knot

Arbor knot—method 2

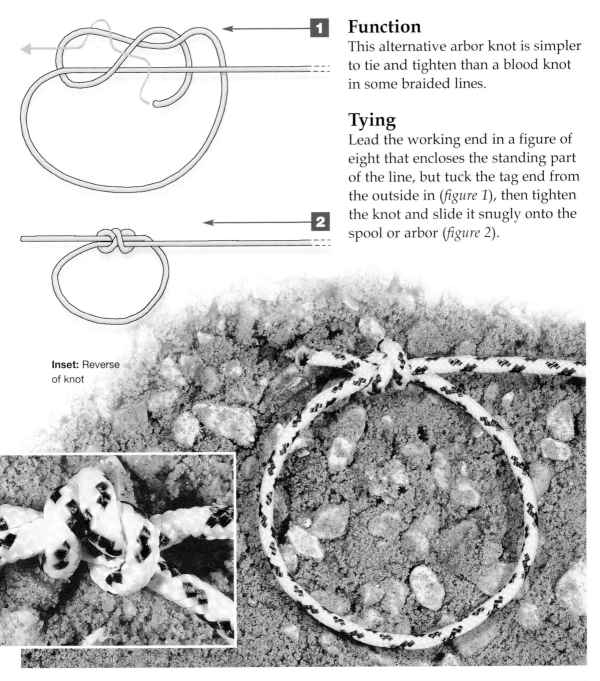

1

Function

This alternative arbor knot is simpler to tie and tighten than a blood knot in some braided lines.

Tying

Lead the working end in a figure of eight that encloses the standing part of the line, but tuck the tag end from the outside in (*figure 1*), then tighten the knot and slide it snugly onto the spool or arbor (*figure 2*).

2

Inset: Reverse of knot

Crawford knot

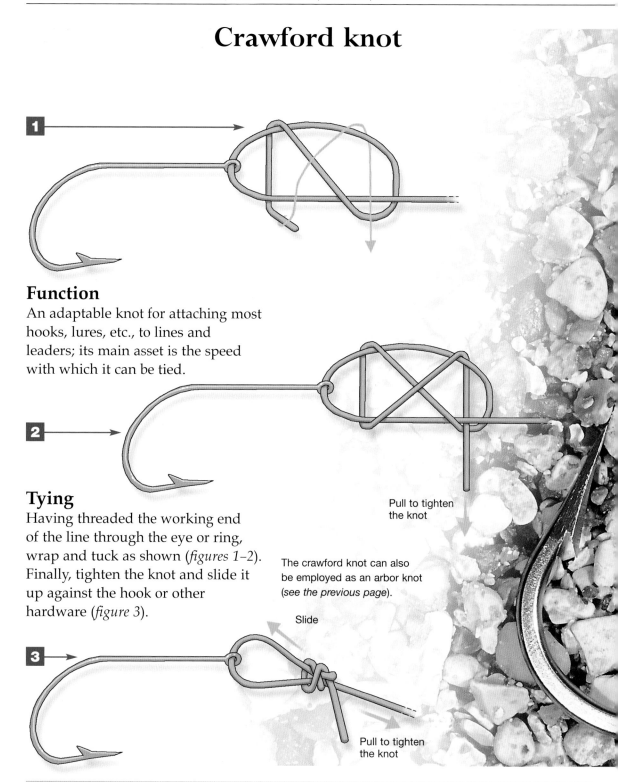

Function
An adaptable knot for attaching most hooks, lures, etc., to lines and leaders; its main asset is the speed with which it can be tied.

Tying
Having threaded the working end of the line through the eye or ring, wrap and tuck as shown (*figures 1–2*). Finally, tighten the knot and slide it up against the hook or other hardware (*figure 3*).

Pull to tighten the knot

The crawford knot can also be employed as an arbor knot (see *the previous page*).

Slide

Pull to tighten the knot

Reverse of knot

Non-slip mono knot

Function

A small fixed loop is preferable to one that slips snugly up against the eye of a hook or lure, since it does not restrict their movement but enables them to dart, flit, and flirt in a lifelike way.

Tying

Tie an overhand knot in the line, then lead the working end through the eye of the lure and back through the knot (re-entering on the same side that it emerged)(*figure 1*). Wrap four turns around the standing part and bring the end back to tuck through the mouth of the initial overhand knot (*figures 2–3*). Tighten the knot and trim the tag end (*figure 4*).

Reverse of knot

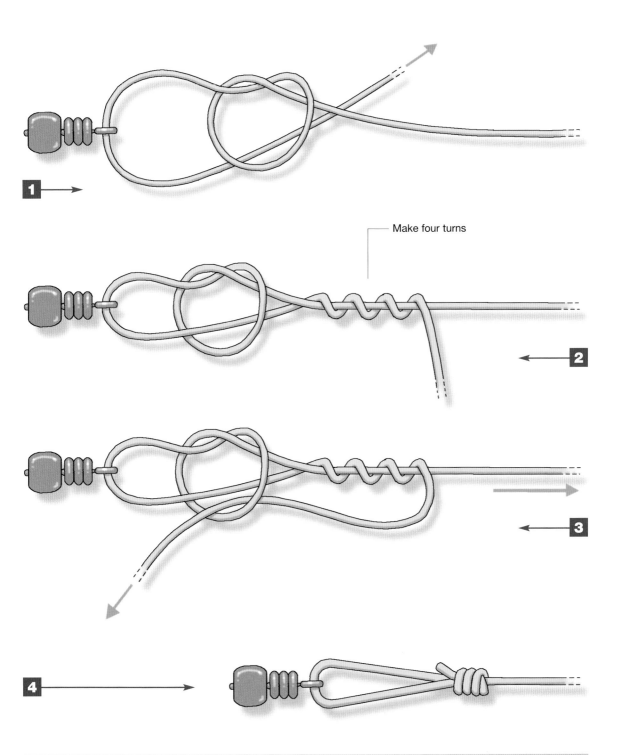

Make four turns

Rapala knot

Function

This knot was promoted by the Rapala company for use with its products to enliven the movement of lures, plugs, and flies attached to it.

Tying

Tie an overhand knot in the line, then pass the working end through the ring and back to re-enter the overhand knot (from the opposite side to which it emerged)(*figure 1*). Wrap three turns around the standing part of the line (*figure 2*). Take the end back through the knot as shown (*figure 3*) and then tuck it through the loop that has been created (*figure 4*). Tighten the knot and trim the tag end (*figure 5*).

Reverse of knot

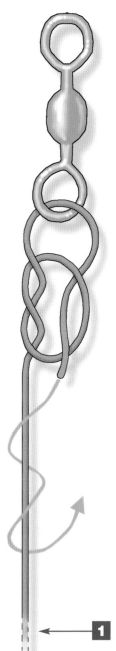

1

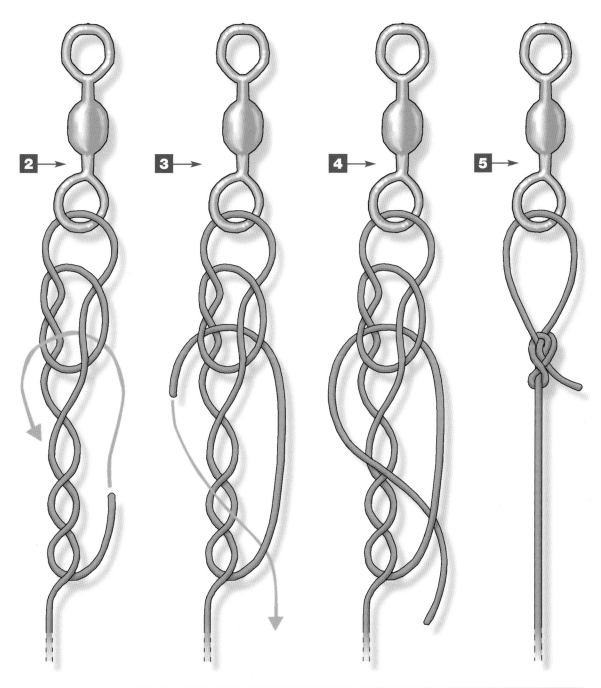

Jansik special

Function

With lighter lines, greater knot strength is achieved by threading the end twice through the ring or eye of the hook or other tackle item.

Tying

Pass the end once, then a second time, through the ring or eye (*figure 1*). Wrap the end (going away from the hook or lure) to enclose both turns plus the standing part of the line (*figure 2*). Pull the knot tight and trim off the tag end (*figure 3*).

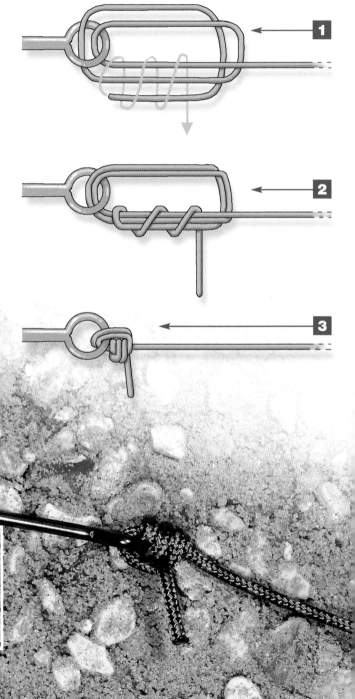

Reverse of knot

World's Fair knot

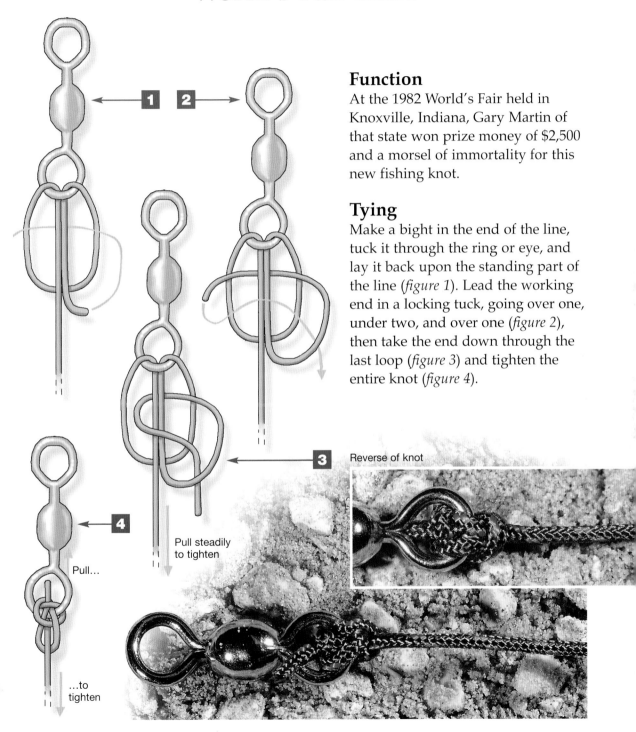

Function
At the 1982 World's Fair held in Knoxville, Indiana, Gary Martin of that state won prize money of $2,500 and a morsel of immortality for this new fishing knot.

Tying
Make a bight in the end of the line, tuck it through the ring or eye, and lay it back upon the standing part of the line (*figure 1*). Lead the working end in a locking tuck, going over one, under two, and over one (*figure 2*), then take the end down through the last loop (*figure 3*) and tighten the entire knot (*figure 4*).

Reverse of knot

Pull steadily to tighten

Pull...

...to tighten

Palomar knot

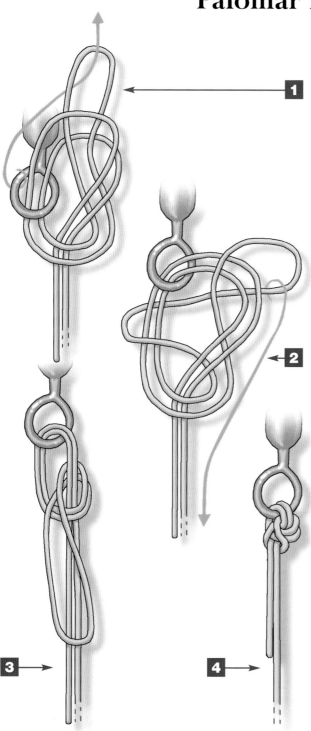

Function

1

This is one of the stronger knots. Being somewhat bulky, it is best tied to large single hooks (rather than triple ones which can snag in the tying process). Requiring a long-ish loop or bight, it tends to consume more of a leader line than some other knots.

Tying

Pass the end of the loop or bight through the ring or eye and tie it in an overhand knot (*figure 1*). Tuck the hook, swivel, or whatever through the bight or loop (*figure 2*), which must then be pulled down around the standing part of the line (*figure 3*). Tighten the knot (*figure 4*).

Reverse of knot

Triple palomar knot

Function

This knot is recommended for tying the latest high-tech, so-called super lines to metal rings and hooks. It is strong, highly slip-resistant, and can be tied in fairly heavy lines.

Tying

Pass the end of a long bight or loop through the eye of the hook to create a loop (*figure 1*). Repeat the process twice more (*figure 2*). Tighten the trio of loops just formed around the eye and then tie a half-knot with the end of the bight and the standing part of the line (*figure 3*). Pass the hook through the bight (or the bight over the hook)(*figure 4*); then tighten the knot so that the bight rides over the knot and ends up around the standing part of the line (*figure 5*). Tighten and trim the tag end.

1

Reverse of knot

2

3

4

5

Clinch knot
(also known as a half-blood knot or stevedore knot)

Function
This most basic of the clinch-knot family is best tied with five turns in medium line, but, to avoid problems in tightening it, use only three to four turns in heavy lines.

Tying
Pass the end through the ring or eye and then wrap the required number of turns around the standing part of the line (*figure 1*). Bring the end back toward the hook or other item of tackle and tuck it through the retaining loop before tightening the knot and trimming the tag end (*figure 2*).

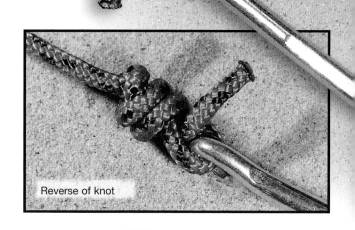

Reverse of knot

1

2

Clinch on shank

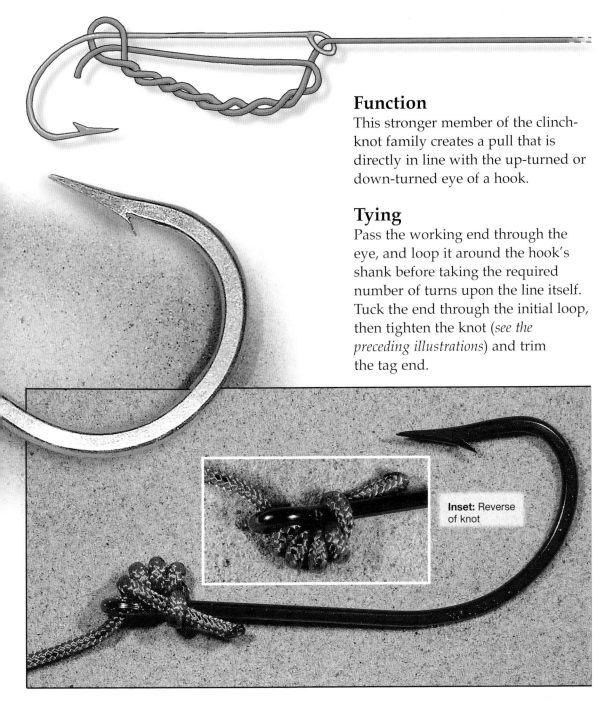

Function

This stronger member of the clinch-knot family creates a pull that is directly in line with the up-turned or down-turned eye of a hook.

Tying

Pass the working end through the eye, and loop it around the hook's shank before taking the required number of turns upon the line itself. Tuck the end through the initial loop, then tighten the knot (*see the preceding illustrations*) and trim the tag end.

Inset: Reverse of knot

Double clinch knot

Function

In a fine line or leader, tie the clinch knot doubled.

Tying

First, make a long bight in the working end of the line and then tie the knot (*figure 1*). Tighten and trim it (*figure 2*).

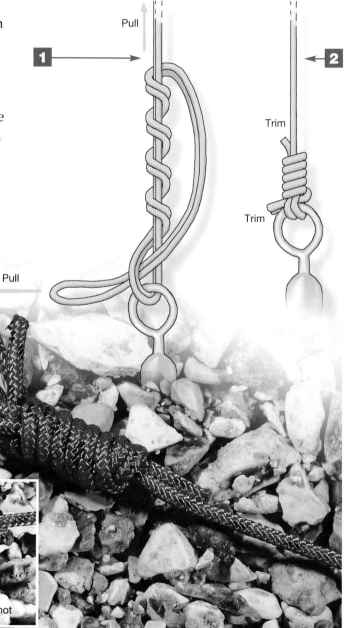

Reverse of knot

Improved clinch knot

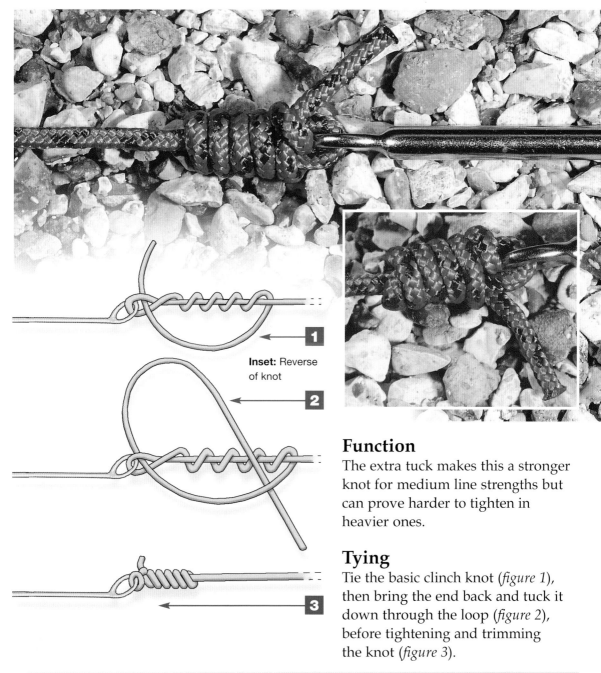

Inset: Reverse of knot

Function

The extra tuck makes this a stronger knot for medium line strengths but can prove harder to tighten in heavier ones.

Tying

Tie the basic clinch knot (*figure 1*), then bring the end back and tuck it down through the loop (*figure 2*), before tightening and trimming the knot (*figure 3*).

Improved double clinch knot

Function

In the thinnest lines, use this doubled version of the improved clinch knot.

Tying

Make a long bight in the end of the line and then tie the knot (*figure 1*). Tighten and trim it (*figure 2*).

Reverse of knot

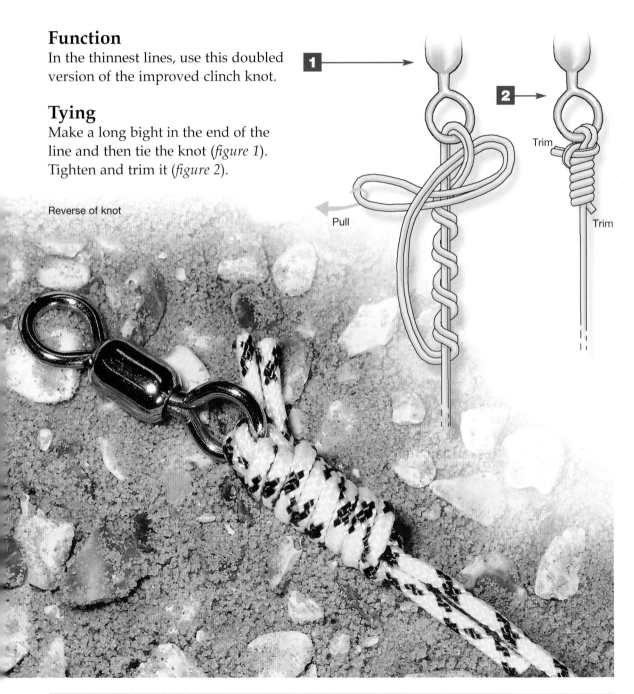

Pull

Trim

Trim

Swivel knot

(also known as the Cairnton or Woods knot)

Front of knot

Function

Knots used as swivel knots, while attached to the shank of a ring or eye, must not impair the action of the swivel. It is also an accepted knot to attach a line to a fly because, tied around the hook's shank, it creates a straighter pull.

Tying

Pass the end through the eye or ring, then wrap and tuck as shown (*figure 1*). Push the second loop over the eye or ring, to rest snugly alongside the first one, and tighten the knot (*figures 2–3*).

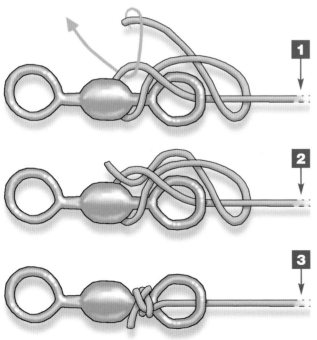

1

2

3

Reverse of knot

Hook or swivel braid knot

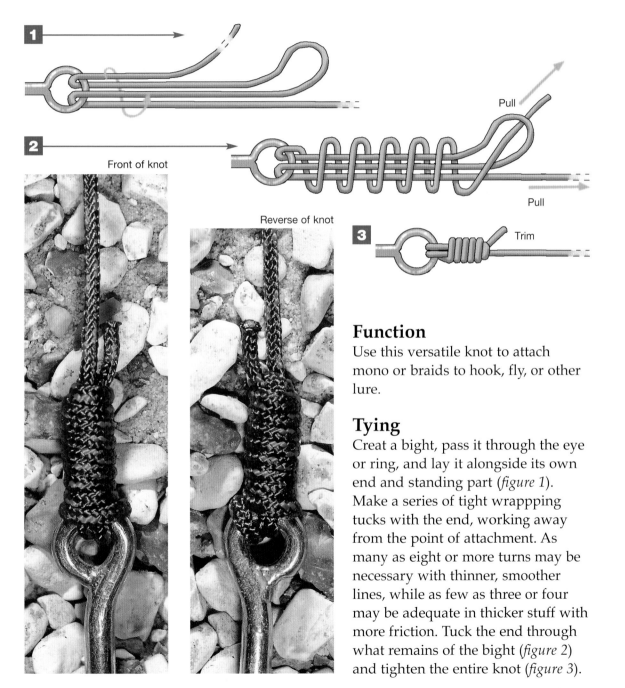

Front of knot

Reverse of knot

Pull

Pull

Trim

Function

Use this versatile knot to attach mono or braids to hook, fly, or other lure.

Tying

Creat a bight, pass it through the eye or ring, and lay it alongside its own end and standing part (*figure 1*). Make a series of tight wrappping tucks with the end, working away from the point of attachment. As many as eight or more turns may be necessary with thinner, smoother lines, while as few as three or four may be adequate in thicker stuff with more friction. Tuck the end through what remains of the bight (*figure 2*) and tighten the entire knot (*figure 3*).

Lock knot

(French: *nœud surrure*)

Function

Knots that are tied to hook shanks usually require an up-turned or down-turned eye; but this knot, which originated in France, was designed purposely to attach monofilament to flat-eyed hooks and yet maintain a pull in line with the shank.

Tying

Hold the standing part of the line alongside the hook's shank, then create a loop (as shown) around the shank and take the end back to tuck down through the eye (*figure 1*). Make four wrapping turns, working away from the eye, before tucking the end through the loop (*figures 2–3*). Carefully tighten the knot and trim off the tag end (*figure 4*).

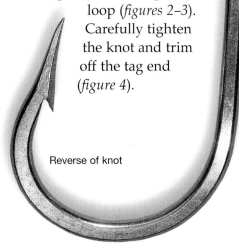

Reverse of knot

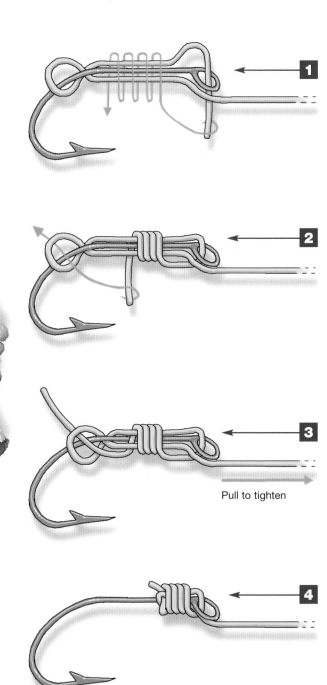

1

2

3

Pull to tighten

4

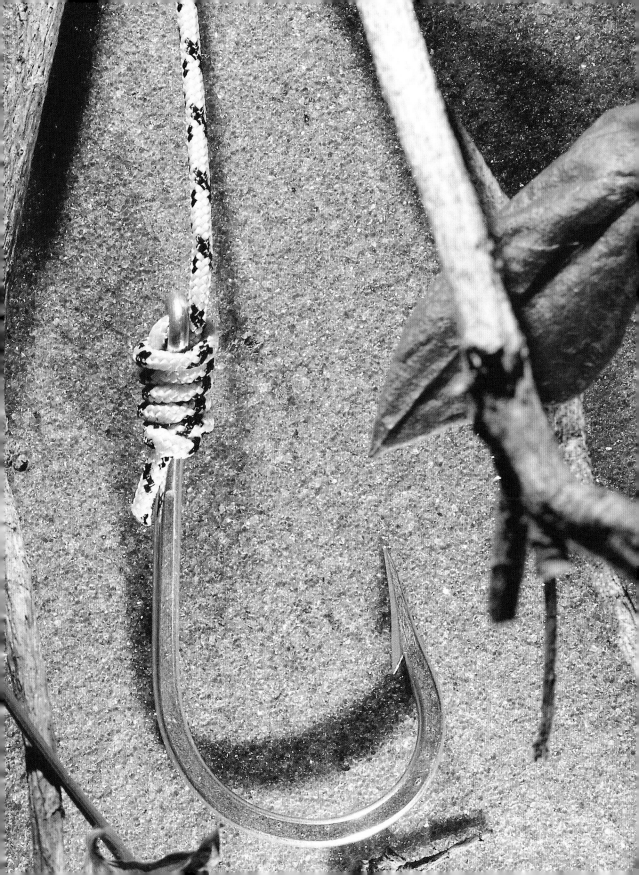

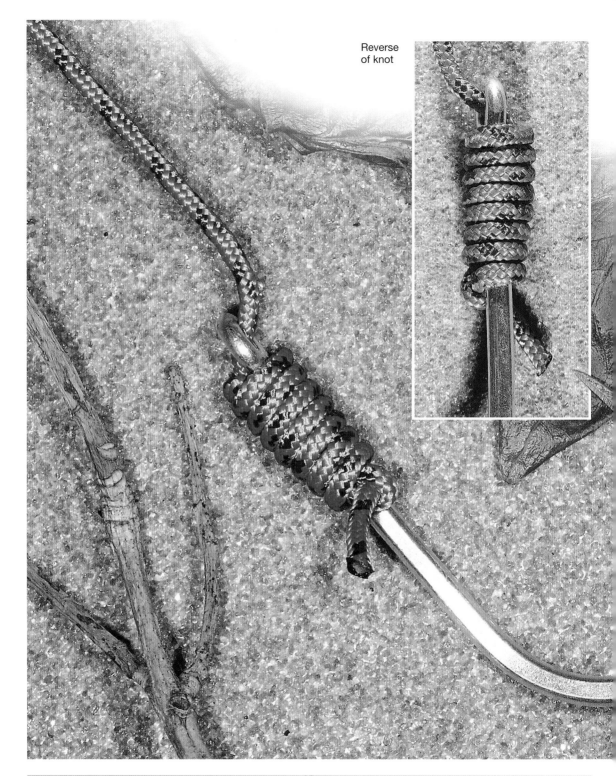

Reverse
of knot

Domhof knot

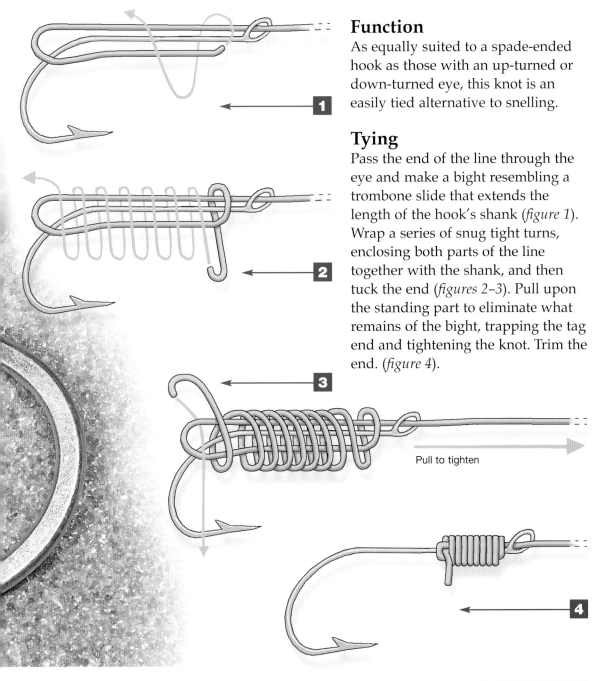

1

2

3

Pull to tighten

4

Function

As equally suited to a spade-ended hook as those with an up-turned or down-turned eye, this knot is an easily tied alternative to snelling.

Tying

Pass the end of the line through the eye and make a bight resembling a trombone slide that extends the length of the hook's shank (*figure 1*). Wrap a series of snug tight turns, enclosing both parts of the line together with the shank, and then tuck the end (*figures 2–3*). Pull upon the standing part to eliminate what remains of the bight, trapping the tag end and tightening the knot. Trim the end. (*figure 4*).

Quick snell knot

Function

"Snelling" is the generic name for a technique, with numerous variations, acquired by sport fishermen from the seagoing professional long-liners. The quick snell is its most basic form.

Tying

Pass the end through the hook's eye, wrap several times around the shank, and bring the end back to trap it beneath the initial wrapping turn (*figure 1*). Tighten and trim (*figure 2*).

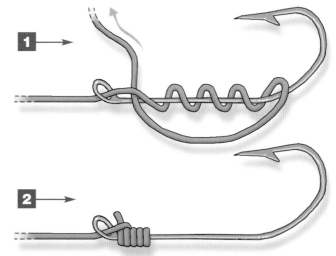

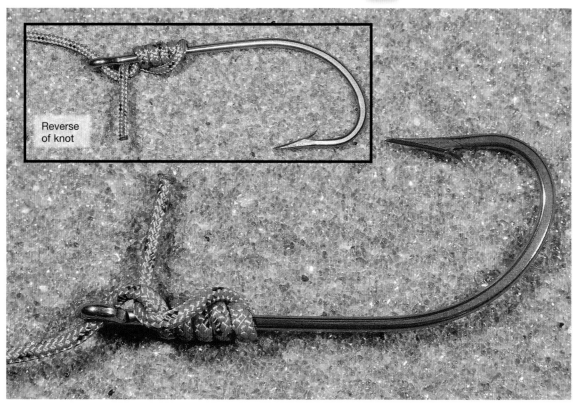

Reverse of knot

Silly snell

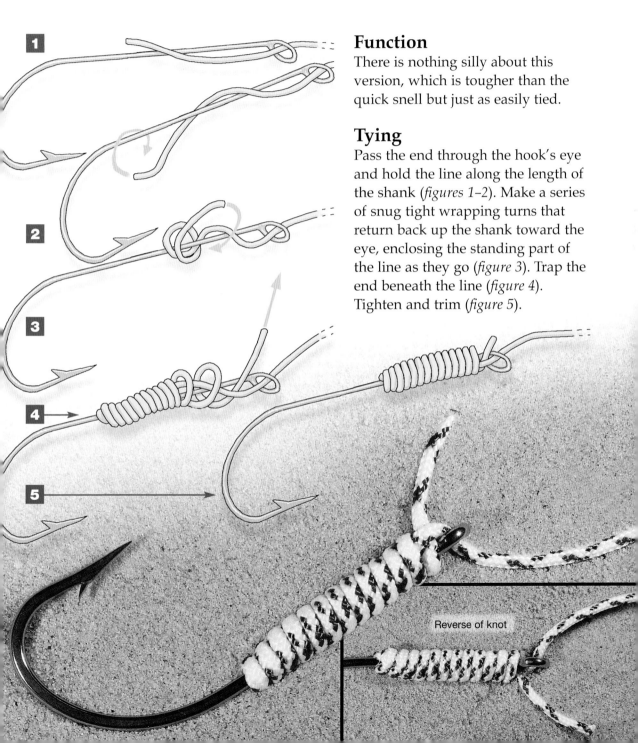

Function

There is nothing silly about this version, which is tougher than the quick snell but just as easily tied.

Tying

Pass the end through the hook's eye and hold the line along the length of the shank (*figures 1–2*). Make a series of snug tight wrapping turns that return back up the shank toward the eye, enclosing the standing part of the line as they go (*figure 3*). Trap the end beneath the line (*figure 4*). Tighten and trim (*figure 5*).

Reverse of knot

Basic snell

(also referred to as a salmon hook knot)

Function

Snelling dates from the days when spade ended hooks (without eyes) were common; and the qualities of strength and security that made this shank connection reliable then fits it equally well for eyed hooks now.

Tying

Having passed the end through the hook's eye, form a circular loop (*figure 1*) and make a series of snug and tight wrapping turns through it, enclosing both shank and line (*figures 2–3*). Tighten in the form of a distorted blood knot and trim the tag end (*figure 4*).

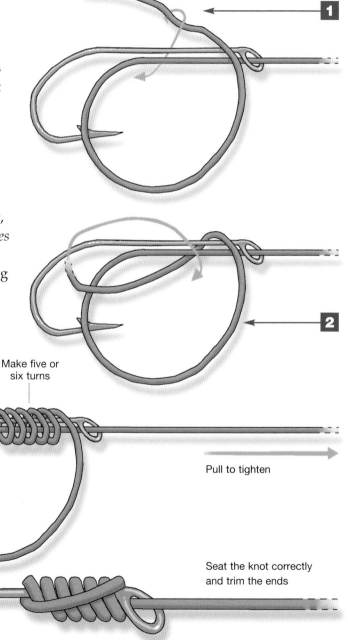

1

2

3

Make five or
six turns

Pull to tighten

Seat the knot correctly
and trim the ends

4

Front of knot

Reverse of knot

Improved basic snell

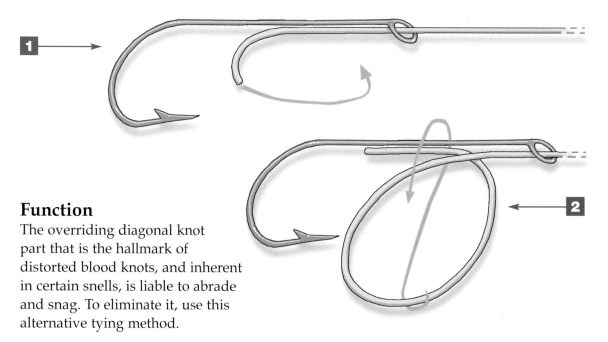

Function

The overriding diagonal knot part that is the hallmark of distorted blood knots, and inherent in certain snells, is liable to abrade and snag. To eliminate it, use this alternative tying method.

Tying

Pass the end through the hook's eye and make a circular loop (*figures 1–2*). Then, using the loop and NOT the end of the line, create a series of snug and tight wrapping turns, enclosing and trapping the tag end alongside the shank of the hook (*figures 3–4*). Finally, secure the knot by pulling on the standing part of the line to eliminate what remains of the shrunken loop (*figure 5*) and trim the end.

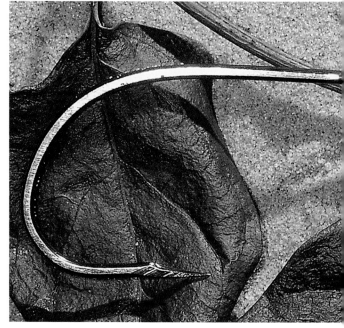

Side view of knot

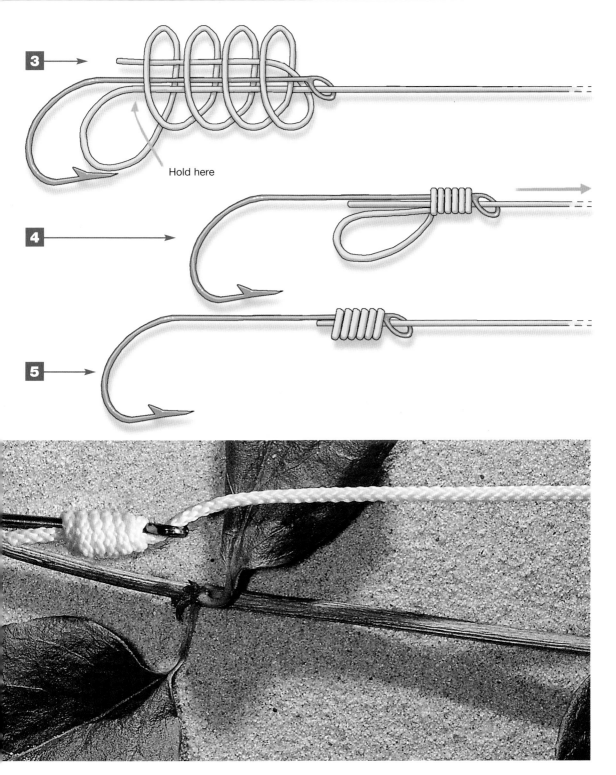

3

Hold here

4

5

Fixed Loops
for Leader Systems

"Loops like the Bimini . . . and others can make your fishing easier, more successful, and more fun."

(Bob McNally—*Fishermen's Knots, Fishing Rigs, and How to Use Them*, 1993)

Relaxing on the river: two anglers fly fishing for salmon on the River Wye, Herefordshire, England.

Angler's loop

(also known as perfection loop)

Function

This is a reliable knot for just about any kind of line or leader with which to start constructing a tackle rig.

Tying

Take a turn with the end of the line, from back to front, around its own standing part (*figure 1*). Repeat the process, tucking the front of the second turn beneath the first one (*figure 2*). Pull the first turn down through the end loop and tighten the knot (*figures 3–4*). To attach a small item of hardware, simply push the loop through the eye or ring and pass the swivel or whatever through it. Arrange the loop around the shank or body of the bit of tackle, and take care it does not ride down over the eye or ring to join the loop legs, which would weaken the attachment (*figure 4*).

Alternative

When the loop is too small to go over the tackle, make the knot a different way. Tie an overhand knot in the line and then pass the end through the ring or eye, bringing it back to reenter the knot on the same side that it left (*figures 5–6*). Wrap and tuck the working end as shown and tighten the knot (*figure 7*).

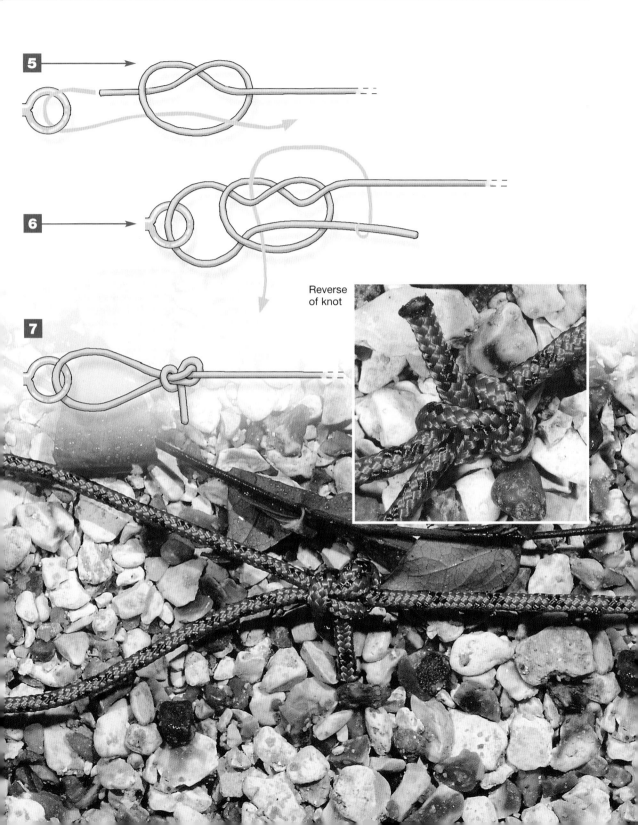

Reverse
of knot

Bimini twist

Function

With a name evocative of Bimini Island in the Bahamas, off the blue water coast of which big game fishing demands tough knots, this knotted loop can be as strong as the unknotted line. Tie it in monofilament or braided line, use it with light or heavy tackle. And—if blue water is out of reach of rod and line, purse or wallet—it works just as well in muddy brown, sea green, or gun-metal gray water.

Tying

Make a long bight and twist into it about 15 turns; fewer for heavy lines, more for the lightest ones (*figures 1–2*). The next stage seems to require three hands, the added help of a foot, and some ingenuity! Anchor the bottom of the loop so that the two loop legs can be forced apart, pushing the turns up; at the same time, brace the standing part of the line vertical, hold the working end at right angles to it, and create a second layer of riding turns, from the top down, over the original ones (*figure 3*). Finish off with a couple of half-hitches (*figure 4*).

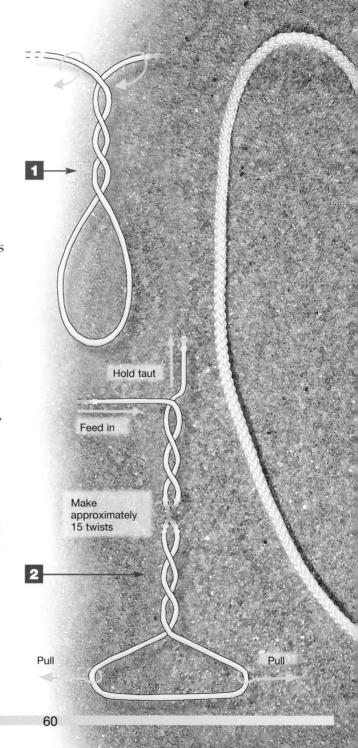

1

Hold taut

Feed in

Make approximately 15 twists

2

Pull

Pull

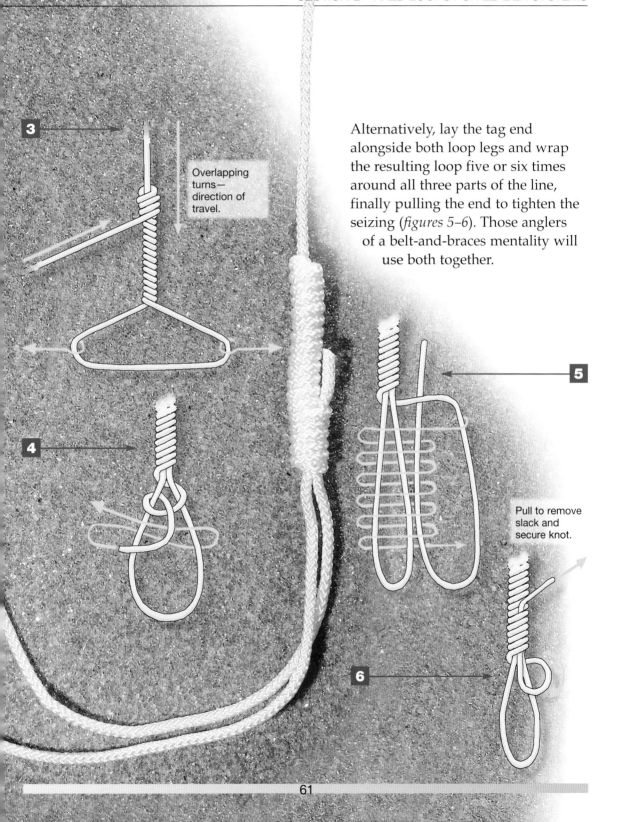

3

Overlapping turns—direction of travel.

4

Alternatively, lay the tag end alongside both loop legs and wrap the resulting loop five or six times around all three parts of the line, finally pulling the end to tighten the seizing (*figures 5–6*). Those anglers of a belt-and-braces mentality will use both together.

5

Pull to remove slack and secure knot.

6

Plaited or braided loop

(also called Australian plait or braid)

Function

This is as strong as a Bimini twist and not as tricky to tie. Use it as the start for any tackle system, light or heavy. While some knots may be rightly regarded as the weak links in an elaborate rig, the plaited character of this knot gives it some stretchiness that may serve as a useful shock-absorber.

Tying

Double, then triple, a long bight of line as shown (*figure 1*). Commence a pigtail plait: go left over middle, then right over middle, repeatedly. See how a loose mirror-image of what is being done at the top appears at the bottom. From time to time, untangle this by removing the tag end (*figures 2–3*). When the loop is the required length, finish off by first laying the tag end up alongside both loop legs, then wrap a series of snug and tight turns around all three parts of the line (*figures 4–5*). Finally, pull the end tight and trim it (*figure 6*).

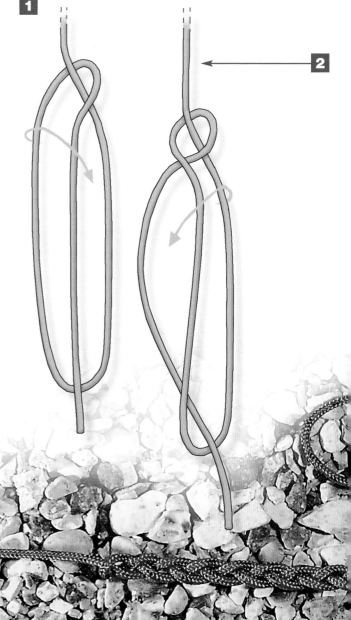

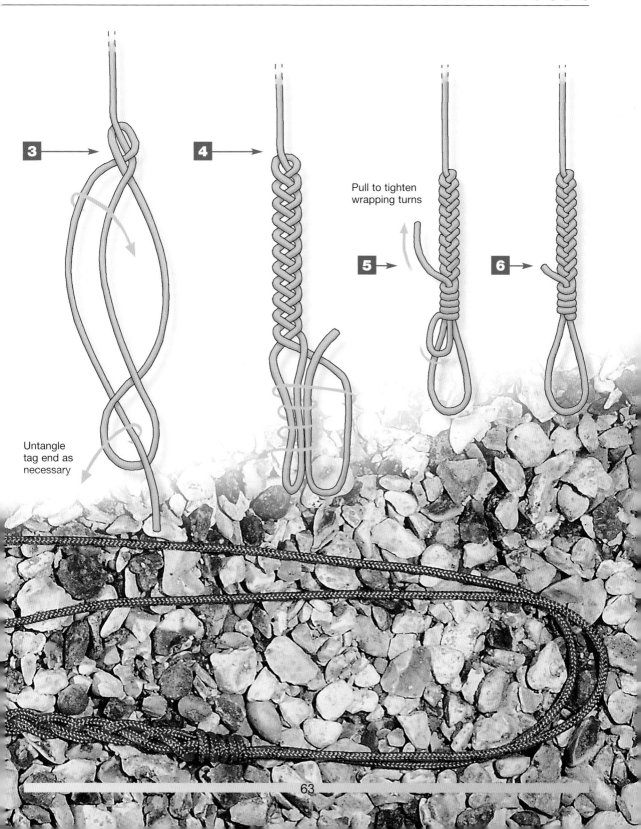

3

Untangle
tag end as
necessary

4

Pull to tighten
wrapping turns

5

6

Surgeon's loop #1
(also known as double overhand loop knot)

Function

This is a fairly strong and secure loop knot, one of the few to emerge from the old days of horsehair, gut, and silk fishing lines, suitable for use in modern monofilaments.

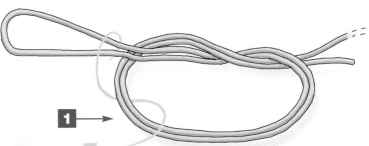

1 →

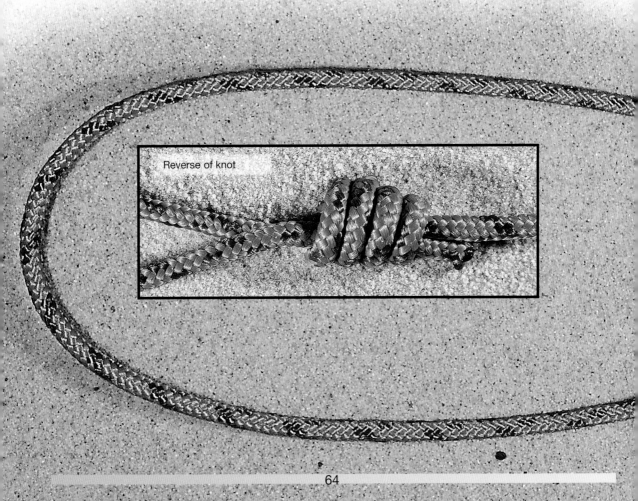

Reverse of knot

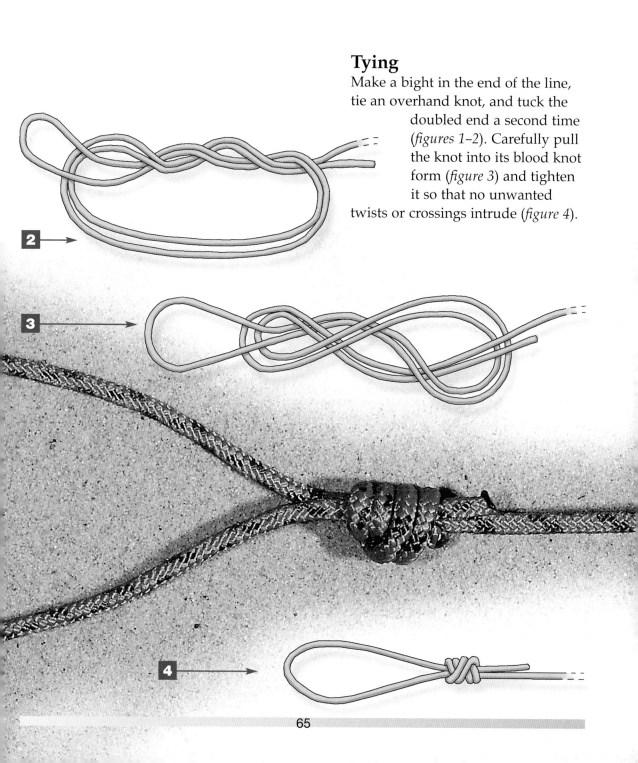

Tying

Make a bight in the end of the line, tie an overhand knot, and tuck the doubled end a second time (*figures 1–2*). Carefully pull the knot into its blood knot form (*figure 3*) and tighten it so that no unwanted twists or crossings intrude (*figure 4*).

Surgeon's loop #2
(also known as triple overhand loop knot)

Function

Extra strength and security result from adding extra turns to a double overhand loop knot. More than the three illustrated and described here result in the knot being known by other names, such as surgeon's loop, thumb loop, and spider's knot or loop.

Reverse of knot

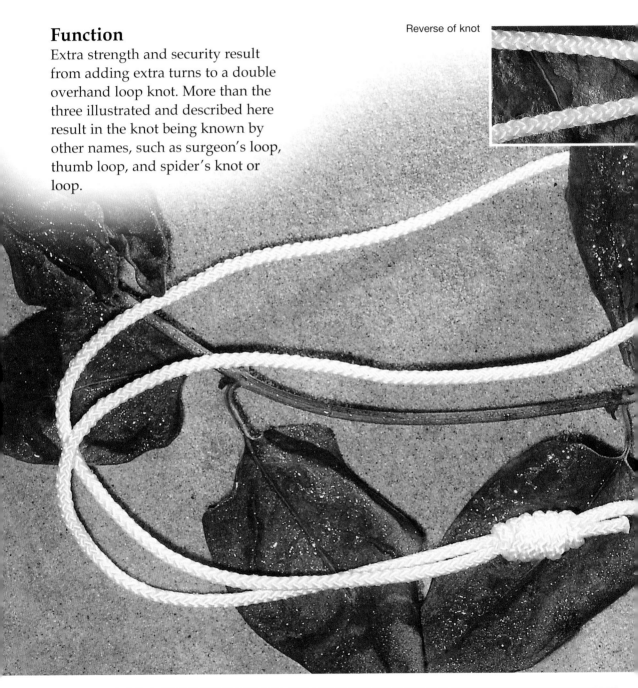

Tying

Make a bight in the end of the line and tie a double overhand knot (*figure 1*). Add an extra tuck before working the knot into its blood knot form and tightening it (*figures 2–3*).

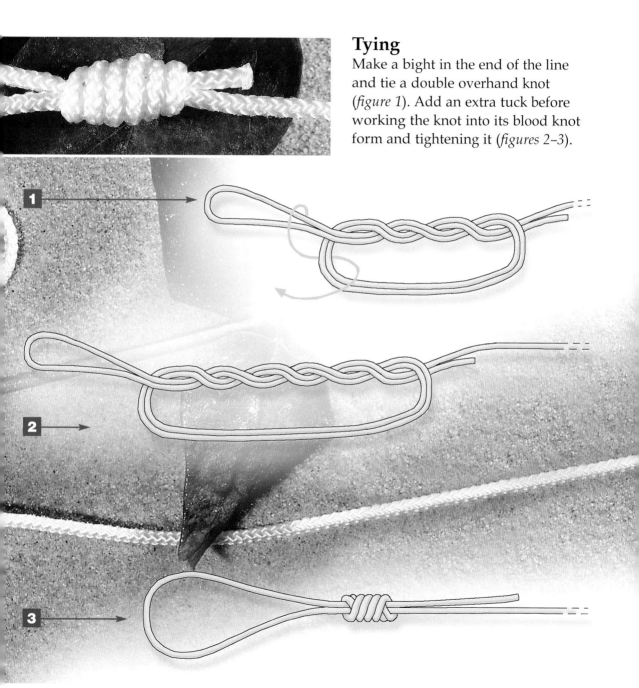

Figure-of-eight loop

Function

For a fixed loop that is quick and easy to tie, use this knot.

Tying

Double the end of the line, form a loop as shown (*figure 1*), then lead the working end of the bight over the standing part and into a locking tuck that creates the required length of loop (*figures 2–3*). Pull tight, taking care to eliminate unwanted twists and crossings that will otherwise weaken the knot.

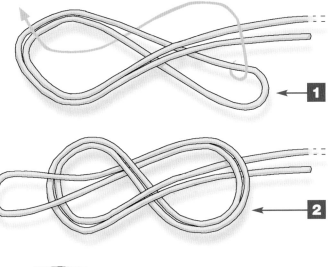

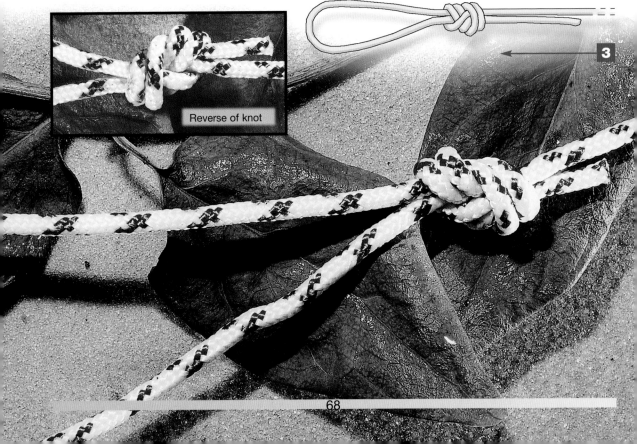

Reverse of knot

Figure-of-eight loop
(double)

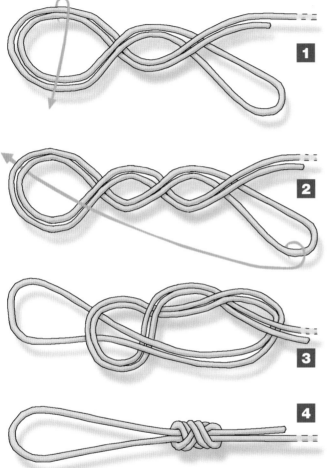

Function

All knots hold due to a subtle combination of friction and nip (either concentrated or diffused). Simplicity is generally achieved at the expense of these desirable properties; while added strength and security usually require extra twists and tucks. This knot will hold in materials that might cause the single figure-of-eight loop to fail.

Tying

Form a long-ish bight in the end of the line, bend it back on itself, and create a couple of interlocking elbows (*figure 1*). Make an extra twist and then tuck the end of the bight through the loop (*figures 2–3*). Tighten the knot, carefully removing all unwanted twists and crossings that would otherwise weaken the knot (*figure 4*).

Figure-of-eight loop
(triple)

Function

This is the end of the series of increasingly strong and secure figure-of-eight loop knots, after which the next step up is the plaited or braided loop or a Bimini twist.

Tying

Begin as if tying a double figure-of-eight loop, but take an extra twist before tucking the end (*figures 1–2*). Tighten as before (*figure 3*).

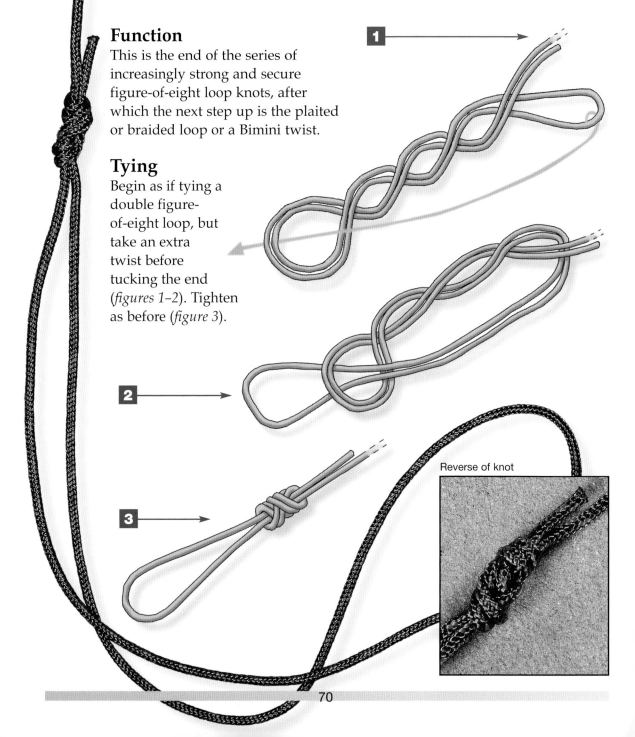

Reverse of knot

Trombone loop

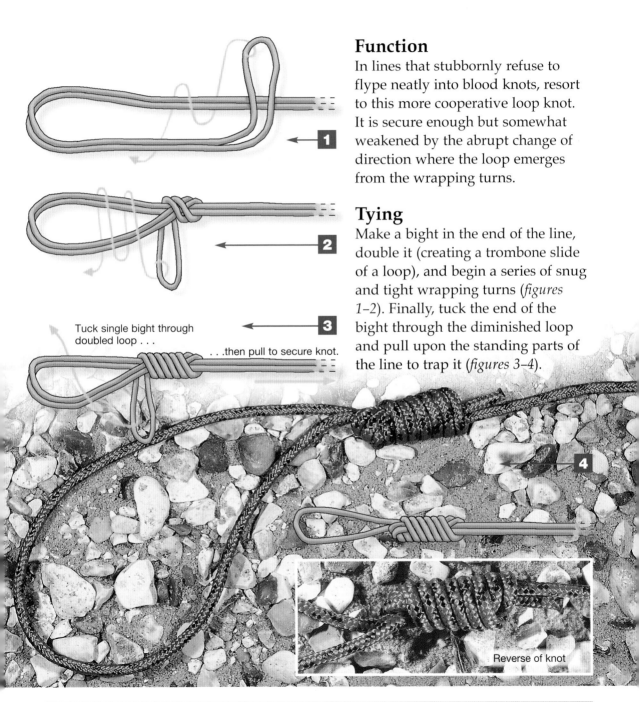

1

2

Tuck single bight through
doubled loop . . .

. . .then pull to secure knot.

3

4

Reverse of knot

Function

In lines that stubbornly refuse to flype neatly into blood knots, resort to this more cooperative loop knot. It is secure enough but somewhat weakened by the abrupt change of direction where the loop emerges from the wrapping turns.

Tying

Make a bight in the end of the line, double it (creating a trombone slide of a loop), and begin a series of snug and tight wrapping turns (*figures 1–2*). Finally, tuck the end of the bight through the diminished loop and pull upon the standing parts of the line to trap it (*figures 3–4*).

Blood knot loop

Function

This ingenious hybrid knot has survived from an earlier angling age and was described by Stanley Barnes in his classic *Anglers' Knots in Gut and Nylon* (1948). Use it to secure a thicker backing line to a loop tied in thinner line.

Tying

Double the loop line, then lay the thicker backing line alongside both loop legs and make at least three wrapping turns (working away from the loop) to enclose all three sections of line (*figure 1*). Tuck the tag end of the backing line up beneath its own standing part, and then begin to wrap the twin loop legs around the backing line as shown (*figure 2*). Finally, tuck them down beneath themselves, to emerge from the resulting knot in the opposite direction to the thicker tag end. Tighten the knot and trim the trio of ends (*figure 3*).

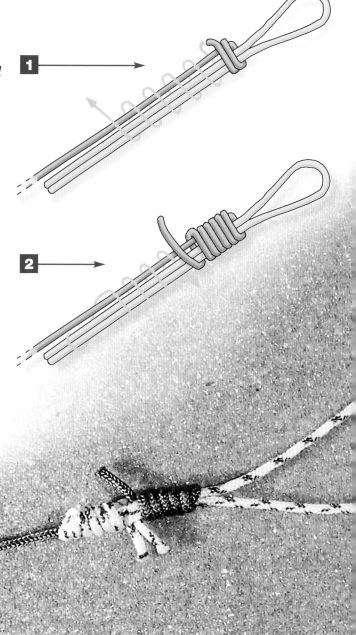

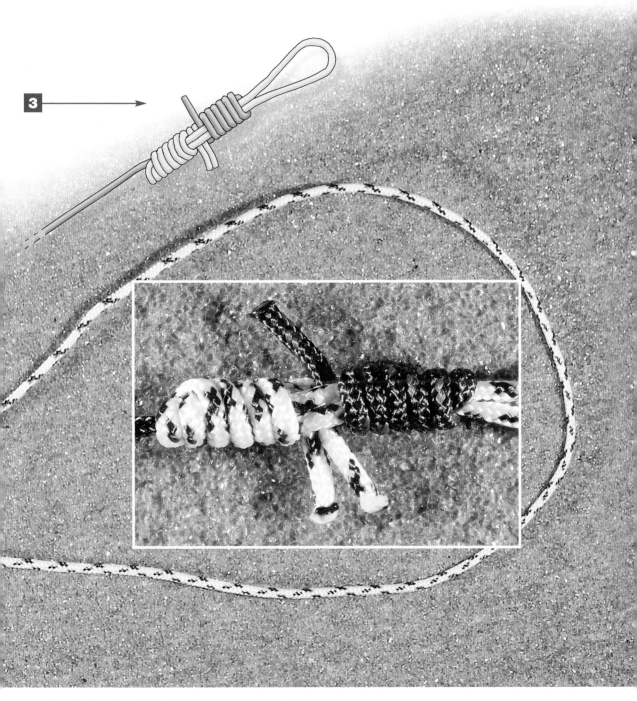

Knots for Joining Lines

"Joining two lines together involves one of the most important aspects of knot building."

(Mark Sosin & Lefty Kreh—
Practical Fishing Knots, 1991)

Coils of lobster trap lines lie on the quayside at Vinalhaven Island, Maine.

Water knot

Function

This veteran of the angling scene is neither as strong nor as secure as a blood knot, but it is quickly and easily tied and will hold in lines of somewhat dissimilar diameter and construction.

Tying

Bring the two ends together, left over right, and tie a half-knot; then cross the two ends, right over left, and tuck each end in turn through the knot parallel to the lead of the other strand (*figures 1–2*). Tighten and trim (*figure 3*).

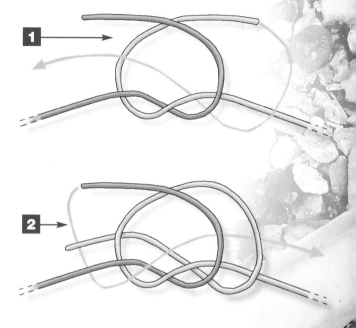

Reverse
of knot

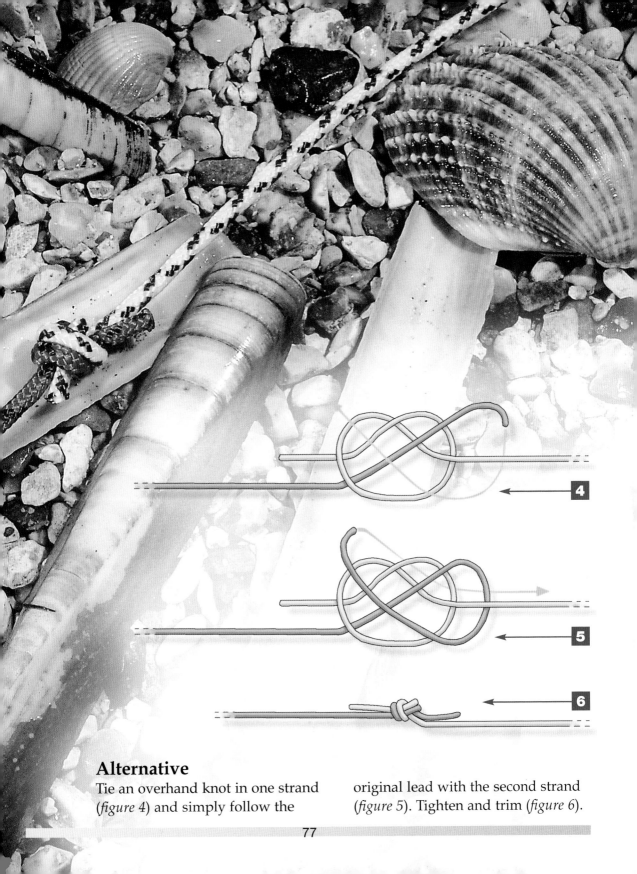

Alternative

Tie an overhand knot in one strand (*figure 4*) and simply follow the original lead with the second strand (*figure 5*). Tighten and trim (*figure 6*).

Surgeon's knot
(also known as the water knot, triple tucked)

Function

In thinner or slicker lines that might break free from the basic water knot, try the added strength and security of this triple-tucked version.

Tying

Lay the two strands together, parallel and pointing in opposite directions, before tying a triple overhand knot (*figures 1–2*). Gradually tighten the knot, transforming it into a blood knot configuration (*figure 3*). Tighten fully and trim (*figure 4*).

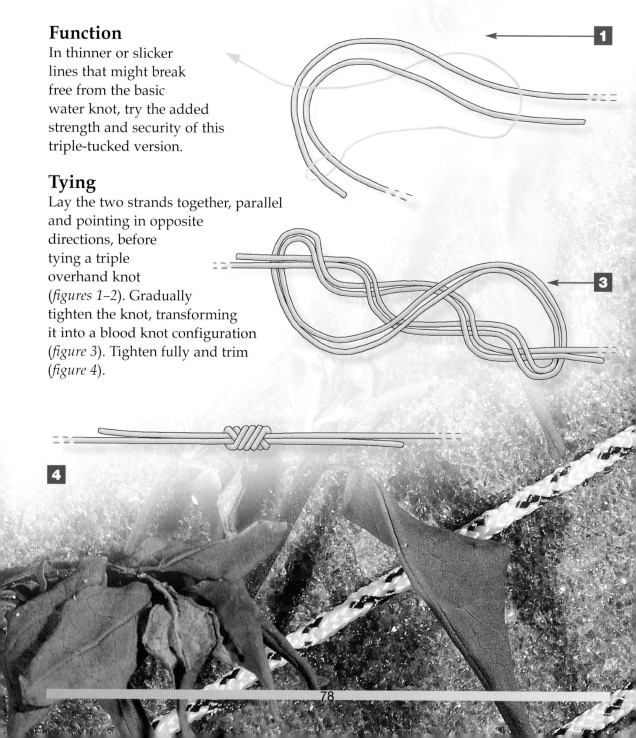

Blood knot, direct
(inward coils)

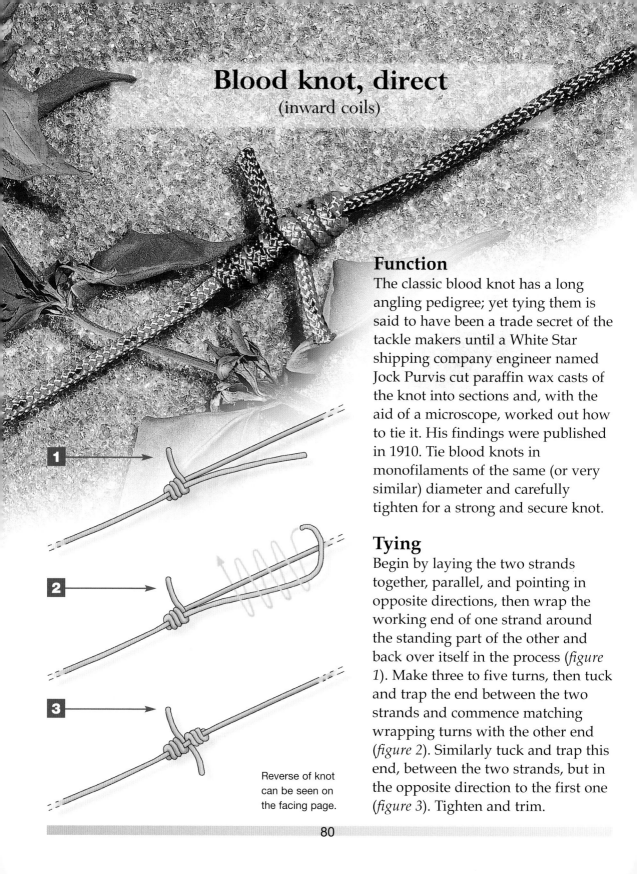

Function

The classic blood knot has a long angling pedigree; yet tying them is said to have been a trade secret of the tackle makers until a White Star shipping company engineer named Jock Purvis cut paraffin wax casts of the knot into sections and, with the aid of a microscope, worked out how to tie it. His findings were published in 1910. Tie blood knots in monofilaments of the same (or very similar) diameter and carefully tighten for a strong and secure knot.

Tying

Begin by laying the two strands together, parallel, and pointing in opposite directions, then wrap the working end of one strand around the standing part of the other and back over itself in the process (*figure 1*). Make three to five turns, then tuck and trap the end between the two strands and commence matching wrapping turns with the other end (*figure 2*). Similarly tuck and trap this end, between the two strands, but in the opposite direction to the first one (*figure 3*). Tighten and trim.

Reverse of knot can be seen on the facing page.

Blood knot, indirect
(outward coils)

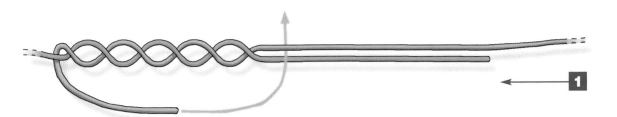

1

Function

This tying method, which requires the ability to flype (*see introduction, pages 11 and 12*), results in the same basic blood knot as before.

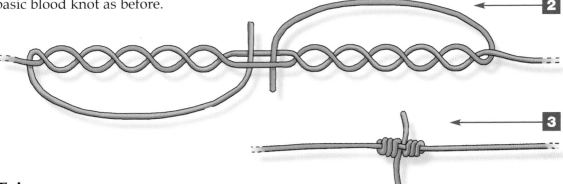

2

3

Tying

Lay the two strands together, parallel and pointing in opposite directions. Wrap three to five turns with one end around the adjacent standing part of the other strand, then bring the end back and tuck it down between the two strands (*figure 1*). Repeat the process with the other end (*figure 2*). Pull steadily upon both standing parts to flype the turns and transform them into the characteristic blood knot form (*figure 3*). Tighten and trim.

Reverse of the blood knot

Reverse of knot

Linfit knot

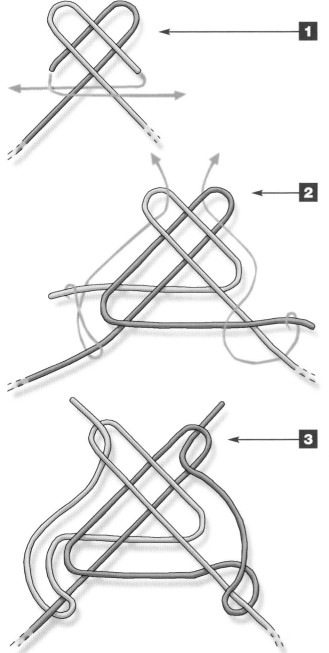

Function

This is a newcomer to the angling repertoire of knots, first published as recently as 1993 by Owen Nuttall of Linthwaite, Huddersfield, in West Yorkshire, England, who came up with it as an alternative to the double fisherman's or grinner knot (*see next page*) for thick, hard, and springy lines. Tying is easier than the two-dimensional illustrations suggest.

Tying

Make a bight in each of the two ends of line to be joined and overlap them as shown (*figure 1*). Take the right-hand working end around the back, and bring the left-hand one across the front (*figure 2*). Then wrap each working end clockwise around the adjacent standing part, and tuck each one (in opposite directions) up through its own initial bight (*figure 3*). Gradually pull the knot tight, allowing it the freedom to settle into its final compact form (*figure 4*). Only then, thoroughly tighten and trim.

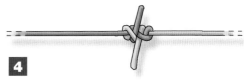

Double fisherman's knot
(also known as a grinner knot)

Function
A strong and secure knot in most materials, this is yet another angling knot to adapt to synthetic fishing lines from the outmoded horsehair, gut and silk ones. Its barrel shape enables it to pass easily through rod guides.

Tying
Lay the two ends together, parallel and pointing in opposite directions, then tie a double overhand knot in one end, enclosing the adjacent standing part (*figures 1–2*). Tighten the knot, turn the work over, and tie an identical double overhand knot with the other end around its companion standing part (*figure 3*). Tighten it too. Finally, pull upon both standing parts to slide the knots together, and trim the tag ends (*figure 4*).

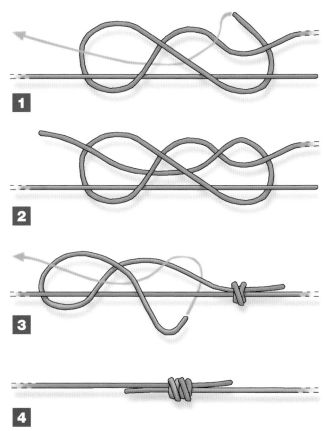

1

2

3

4

Front of knot

Reverse of knot

Triple fisherman's knot
(also known as a double grinner knot)

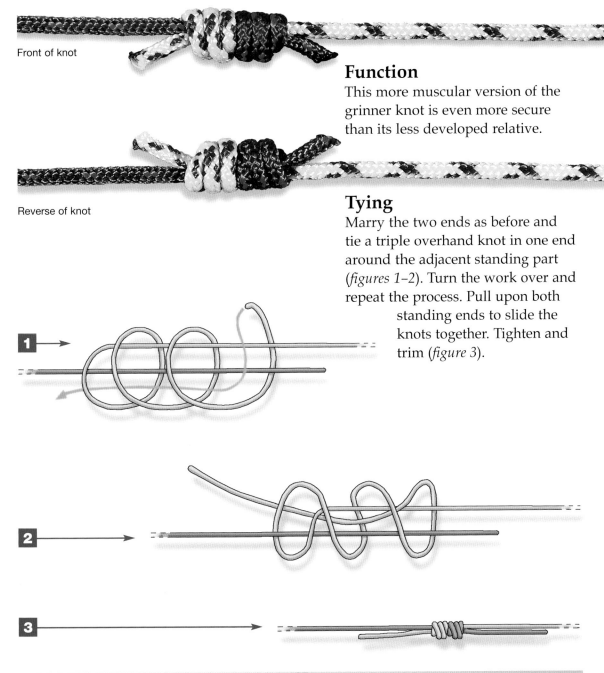

Front of knot

Reverse of knot

Function

This more muscular version of the grinner knot is even more secure than its less developed relative.

Tying

Marry the two ends as before and tie a triple overhand knot in one end around the adjacent standing part (*figures 1–2*). Turn the work over and repeat the process. Pull upon both standing ends to slide the knots together. Tighten and trim (*figure 3*).

1

2

3

Albright knot
(or Albright special)

Function

Jimmy Albright, a guide in the Florida Keys, is credited with inventing, discovering, or popularizing this versatile knot for joining lines of different diameter or construction (backing line to fly line, mono to braid, braid to wire).

Tying

Make a bight in the wire or thicker line. Lay the thinner or more flexible line on top of this bight and then begin to wrap a series of snug and tight turns back along both bight legs with the working end, trapping its own standing part in the process (*figures 1–2*). Finally, tuck the working end through what remains of the diminished bight (*figure 3*). Work the knot tight and either trim the tag end (*figure 4*) or tie it to the standing part of the line.

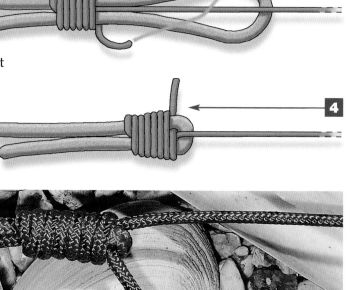

Reverse of knot

Interlocked loops
(method 1, direct)

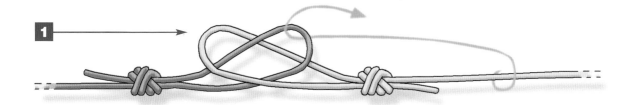

Function

Lines of very different sizes and
constructions can be securely joined
by means of interlocking loops.

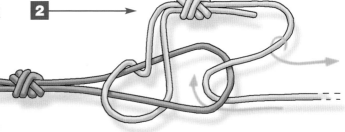

Tying

The quickest and simplest way is to
tuck one loop through the other
(*figure 1*), and then pull its
companion line completely through
it (*figures 2–3*).

Interlocked loops
(method 2, indirect)

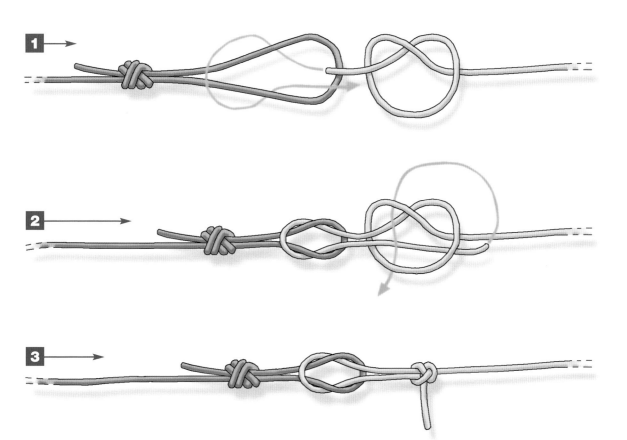

The three component parts can be as tight as the illustrations above or as loose as suggested in the photograph below.

Function
When both lines to be joined are too long or tackle rigs too cumbersome for method 1, this indirect approach becomes necessary.

Tying
Tie an overhand knot in one end and then lead it through a pre-tied loop (*figure 1*). Finally, complete an angler's knot as shown (*figures 2–3*).

Interlocked loops
(method 3, criss-cross)

Function

The introduction of polyethylene gelspun fishing lines, sometimes referred to as "super lines," has generated a need for different tying techniques and rig strategies. This is one response, credited to salt water fly fisherman Rod Harrison and published in 1999 by Geoff Wilson.

Tying

Having interlocked two loops, pull out the gelspun one and impart half a twist to it (*figures 1, 2, 3*). Pass the other end down through it (*figures 4–5*). Repeat the process twice more (*figure 6*).

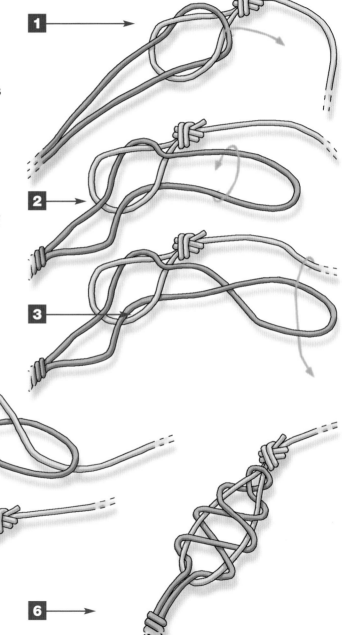

Close up of knot

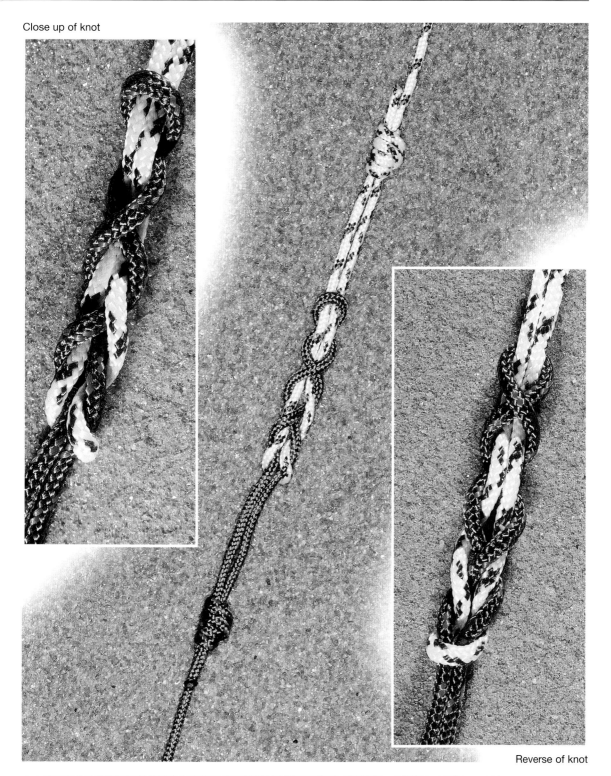

Reverse of knot

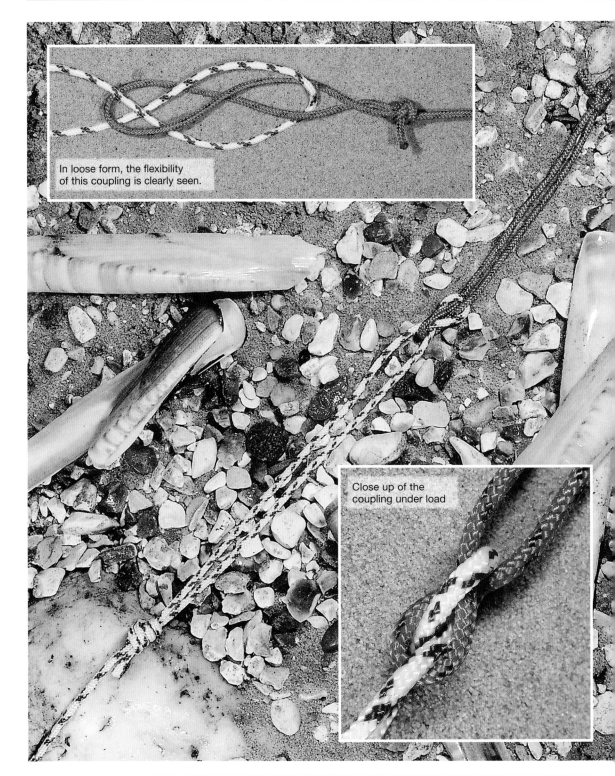

In loose form, the flexibility of this coupling is clearly seen.

Close up of the coupling under load

Interlocked loops
(method 4, carrick bend)

Function

The flat knot, similar to the square (or reef) knot that results from methods 1 and 2, is not ideal as a universal coupling. This modified knot, like a couple of chain links, is more flexible.

Tying

Pass the working end of one line through a pre-tied loop in the other, as shown, tying a single carrick bend (*figures 1–2*). Tie the end to its own standing part with any preferred knot (*figure 3*).

Knot tag end to the standing part of the line.

Plaited interlocked loops

Function

Interlocked loops are secure but may be weaker than the knots forming the loops. This plaited knot creates some shock-absorbing stretchiness.

Side view of knot

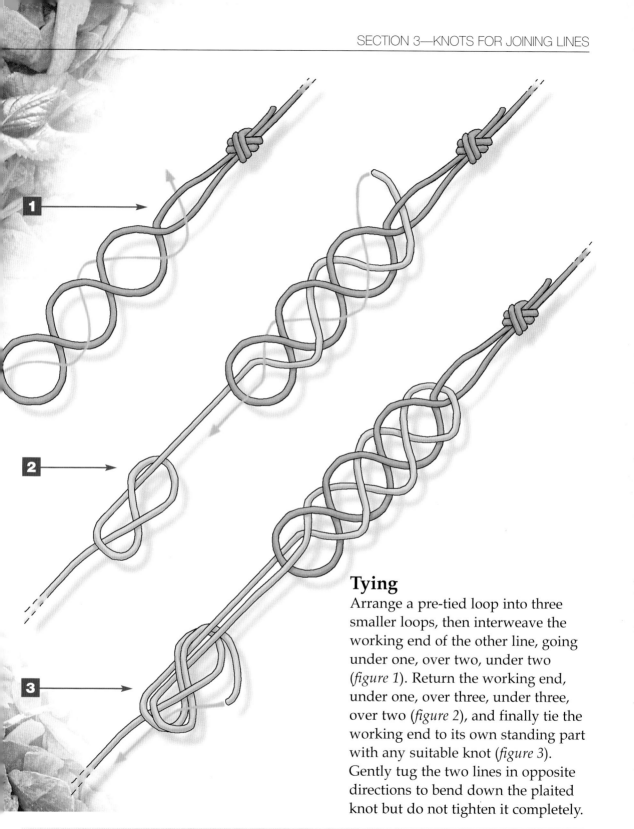

Tying

Arrange a pre-tied loop into three smaller loops, then interweave the working end of the other line, going under one, over two, under two (*figure 1*). Return the working end, under one, over three, under three, over two (*figure 2*), and finally tie the working end to its own standing part with any suitable knot (*figure 3*). Gently tug the two lines in opposite directions to bend down the plaited knot but do not tighten it completely.

Plaited or braided splice

(also called the Australian plaited or braided splice)

Function

For inherent strength, security, and shock-absorbing stretch, this elaborate splice is recommended.

Tying

Form a bight in one working end and arrange it like a collar around the other working end (*figure 1*). Commence a pigtail plait, bringing the right-hand strand over the middle one, then the left-hand over the middle, and right over middle once more (*figures 2–3*). Continue, left over middle, right over middle, for several inches, then bend the middle strand back into a bight and carry on plaiting with two single strands plus the doubled end (*figures 4, 5, 6, 7*). Note how the edge of the plait is made neater if a half-twist is imparted, alternately clockwise and counter-clockwise, each time the doubled strand is at the outside of the plait. (*Continued on next page.*)

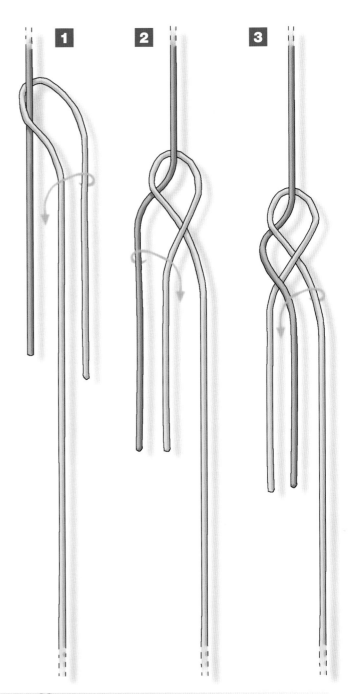

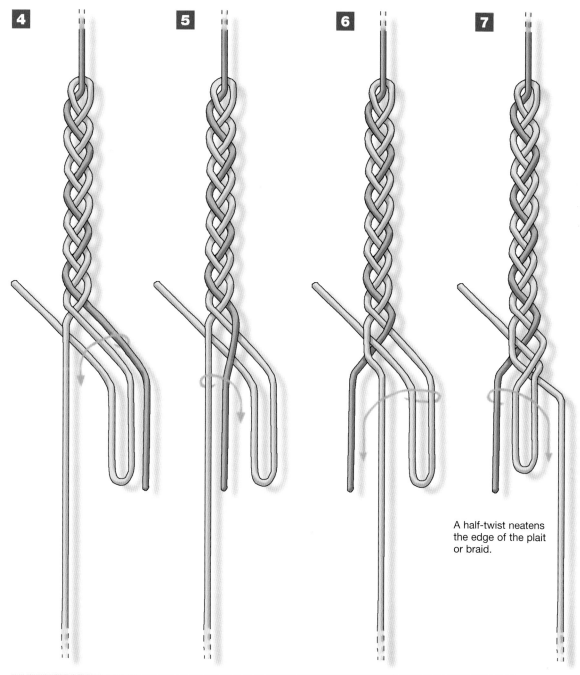

A half-twist neatens
the edge of the plait
or braid.

Finally, make a locking tuck through the diminished bight and ensure that both ends are tightly trapped within the plait (*figures 8–9*).

8

Half-twist

Half-twist

Half-twist

9

Pull to secure
other tag end.

Knots for Fly Fishing

"A good sound knot is every bit as important as the line or lure you select."

(Charles Jardine—*The Pocket Guide to Fishing Knots*, 1998)

Fly-fishing gear

Specialist fly knot

Function

This is a kissing cousin of the clinch knot family. Promoted in the first instance by the Berkley Tackle Company, of Spirit Lake, Indiana, for use by fly fishers, it has proved just as effective with plugs and some other artificial baits.

Tying

Pass the end of the leader through the hook eye of the fly and double the working end into a long bight. Wrap four turns around both legs of the bight, then tuck the working end back through the loop nearest to the fly (*figure 1*). Tighten the knot, locate the resulting noose around the shank, and close it up alongside the eye (*figures 2–3*).

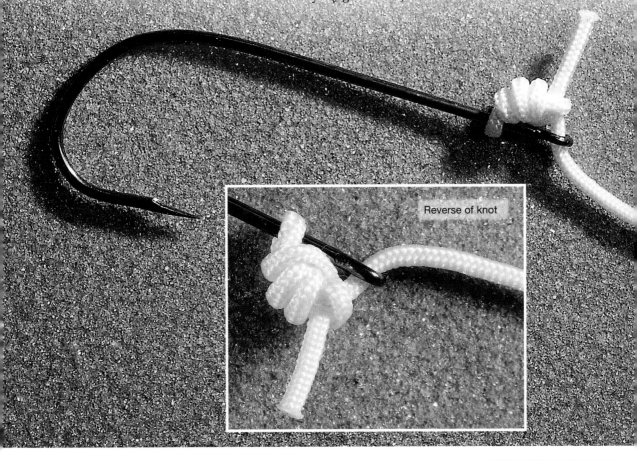

Reverse of knot

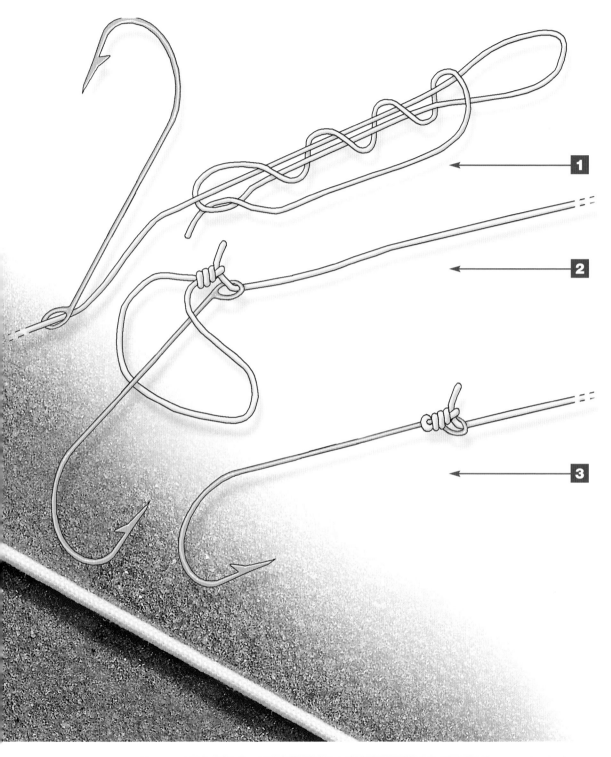

Trilene knot
(also known as the Berkley Trilene knot)

Function

Another offshoot of the clinch family, this knot is made stronger by having two turns through the eye of the hook, but it is not capable of being tied to very small hooks. It can be troublesome to tighten in lines of more than about 12 lbs (5.5 kgs).

Tying

Pass the working end twice through the eye of the hook, take four turns with it around the standing part, then finally bring the end back and tuck it through the two initial turns on the eye (*figure 1*). Flype to tighten.

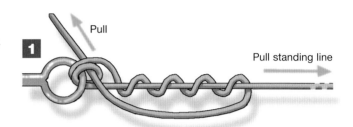

Pull

Pull standing line

Trim

Reverse of knot

Improved Trilene knot

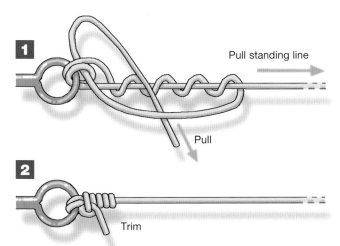

1

Pull standing line

Pull

2

Trim

Function

Akin to the improved clinch knot, it is no stronger than the basic Trilene knot but the extra tuck gives added security.

Tying

Tie a Trilene knot and simply tuck the working end back through the large loop (*figure 1*) before flyping and tightening the knot (*figure 2*).

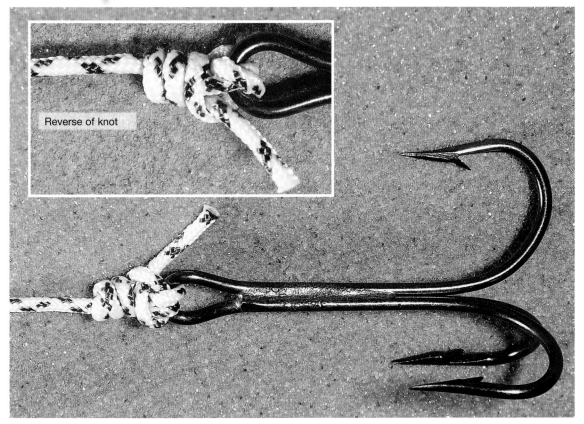

Reverse of knot

Turle knot

Function

This vintage knot dates back to at least 1841 when it was made popular by a Major Turle of Newton Stacey, England, although he never claimed to have invented it. No more than the simplest of nooses, it is outmoded, but remains the basis for several more robust variants.

Tying

Pass the end of the fly line through the eye of the hook and tie a simple noose (*figure 1*). Locate the noose around the shank, beside the eye (*figures 2–3*), and pull it tight (*figure 4*).

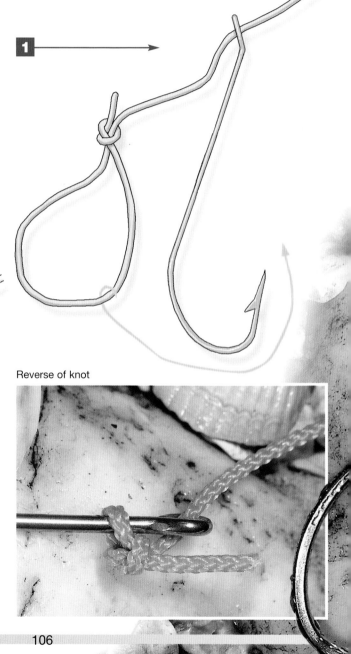

Reverse of knot

Two-turn Turle knot

Function

This stronger version of the Turle knot was first described in the April 1946 issue of *Fishing News*, having been devised and named by the angling author Dr. Stanley Barnes.

Tying

Pass the end of the line through the eye of the fly hook. Form first one, then a second loop, and include both within an overhand knot (*figure 1*). Tuck the hook and lure through both loops and tighten the knot around the shank close to the eye (*figures 2–3*).

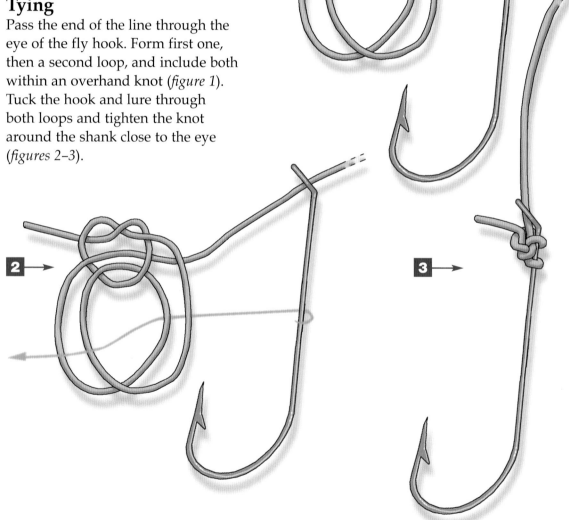

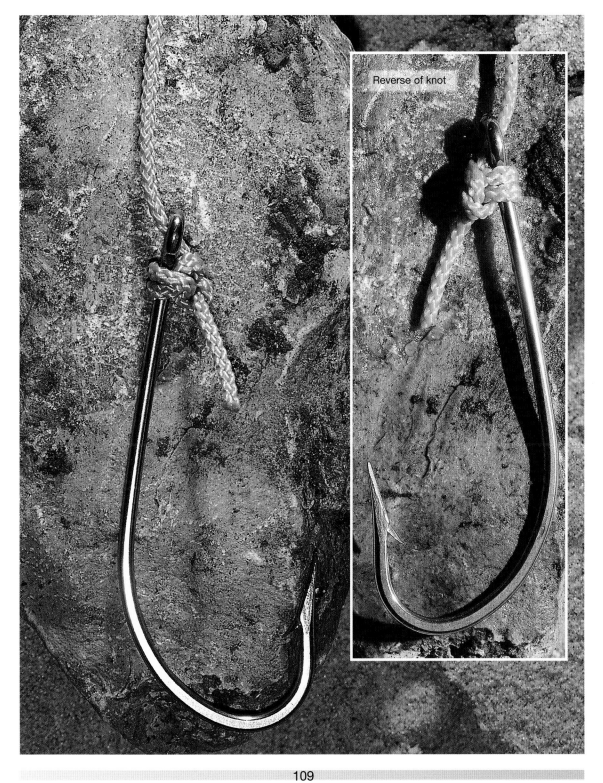

Reverse of knot

Turle knots

(reinforced)

Function

The weakness of both the basic and the double Turle knots lies in their simple overhand knot, both of which may be strengthened and rendered more secure.

Tying

The basic knot may be reinforced by tying a double overhand knot (*figures 1–2*) and, similarly, so may the double one (*figure 3*).

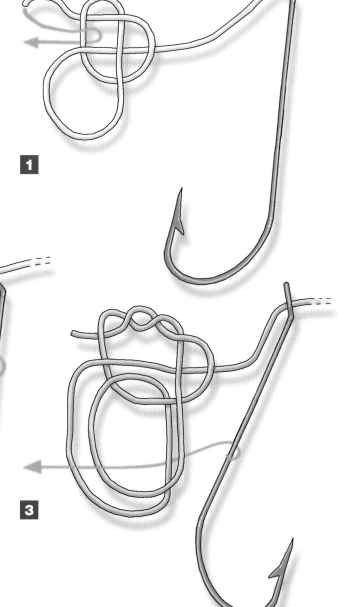

1

2

3

Secured two-turn Turle
knot and, inset above, the
reverse of the knot.

Basic Turle knot secured
and, inset above, the
reverse of the knot.

Nail knot
(also known as the tube knot)

Function

The nail knot joins a fly line to the butt section of the leader, as snelling attaches a line to the shank of a hook. Its name is said to have originated in the 1950s when a noted American fly fisherman named Joe Brooks learned the knot in Argentina using a horseshoe nail. Tying is done more easily, however, by means of a short length of drinking straw, a small diameter metal tube, or even the empty body of a ballpoint pen . . . hence its later name of tube knot.

Tying

Lay the ends of the fly line and backing line together, parallel, pointing in opposite directions, and begin a series of wrapping turns with the end of the backing line to enclose both the fly line plus a nail or tube (*figures 1–2*). Make at least five turns, then withdraw the nail and pass the working end completely through the space it has vacated within the wrapping turns (*figures 3–4*). If using a tube, pass the end through it before withdrawal, when the end will be pulled through at the same time. Tighten slowly so that the wrapping turns bed down neatly alongside one another, and finally tug both ends to tighten (*figure 5*). Trim the tag end.

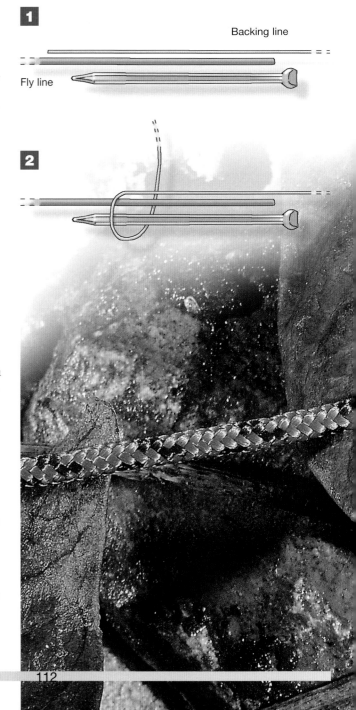

1 Backing line

Fly line

2

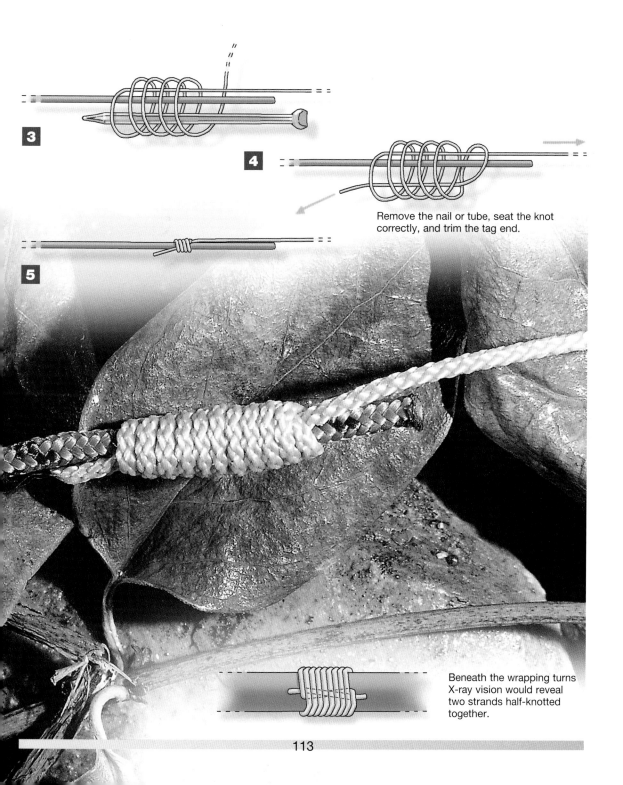

3

4

Remove the nail or tube, seat the knot correctly, and trim the tag end.

5

Beneath the wrapping turns X-ray vision would reveal two strands half-knotted together.

Emergency nail knot

Function

Caught without either nail or tube, a nail knot can be improvised using a bight of spare line to pull the working end through beneath the wrapping turns (not pictured).

Tying

Tie the knot as usual but include within it a bight of line. After the last wrapping turn, tuck the working end through the bight and pull the line out of the knot. Tighten and trim.

Asymmetrical nail knot

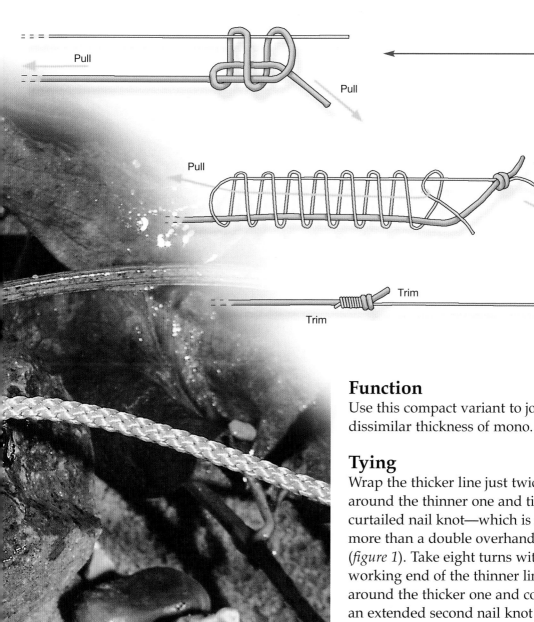

Function

Use this compact variant to join dissimilar thickness of mono.

Tying

Wrap the thicker line just twice around the thinner one and tie a curtailed nail knot—which is nothing more than a double overhand knot—(*figure 1*). Take eight turns with the working end of the thinner line around the thicker one and complete an extended second nail knot (*figure 2*). Work both knots tight, pull them together, and trim the tag ends (*figure 3*).

Conjoined twin nail knots

Function

In game or sport fishing, when maximum strength is required, this knot (which resembles an exceptionally long grinner knot) will join lines of equal thickness or of somewhat dissimilar size.

Tying

Lay the two lines together, parallel and pointing in opposite directions. Using a tube, tie a nail knot of 10 wrapping turns with one end around the adjacent standing part (*figures 1, 2, 3*). Turn the work over and tie a similar nail knot in the other end (*figures 4–5*). Carefully tighten both knots, slide them together, and trim both tag ends (*figure 6*).

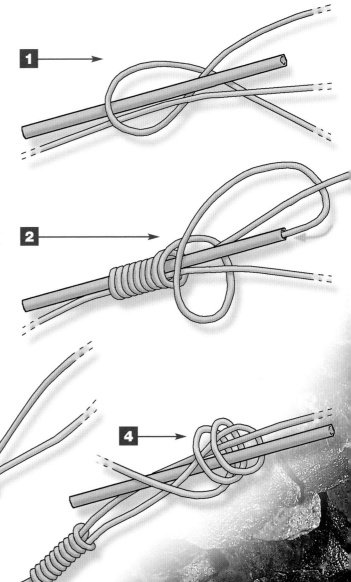

Nail knot loop

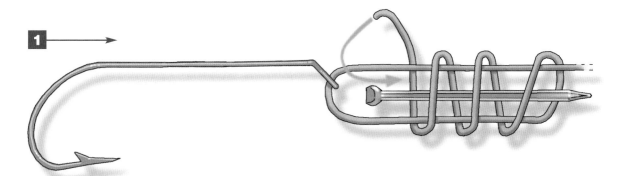

Function

For heavy lines and leaders, such as sea fishing shock tippets, this knot is used. Although it is a sliding noose (commonly known in rope and other cordage as the strangle knot), this tightly tied knot will hold firm enough to maintain a small loop that facilitates the free and realistic movement of a fly or other lure.

Tying

Pass the end of the line or leader through the hook's eye and lay it alongside its own standing part. Wrap and tuck a nail knot, using whatever aid is preferred or available (*figures 1–2*). Tighten the knot and adjust the loop to the required size.

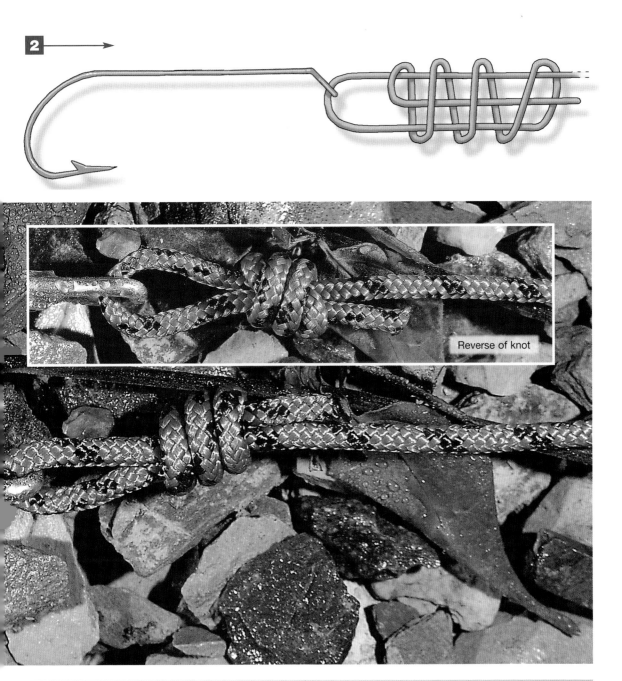

Reverse of knot

A pair of nail knots

Function

Nail knots may be combined in pairs to create a simple seizing, in this instance to form a loop in mono or braid.

Tying

Make a bight in the line and simply tie a couple of basic nail knots following steps 3–5 on pages 112–113.

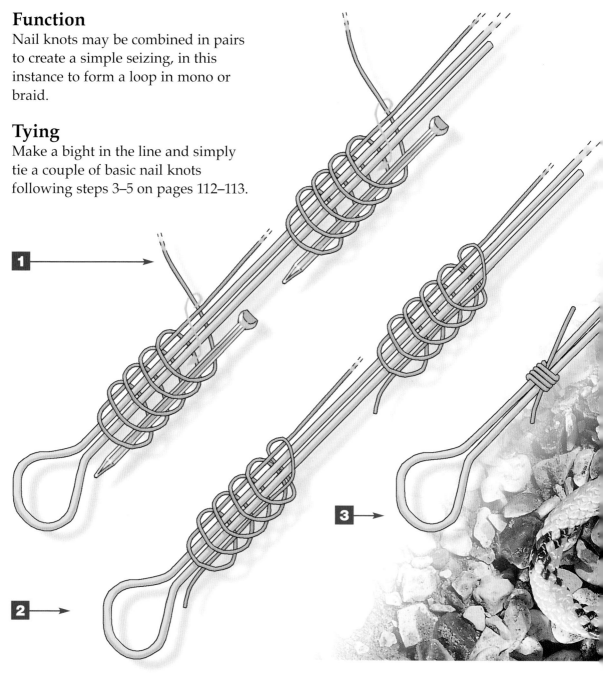

Needle knot

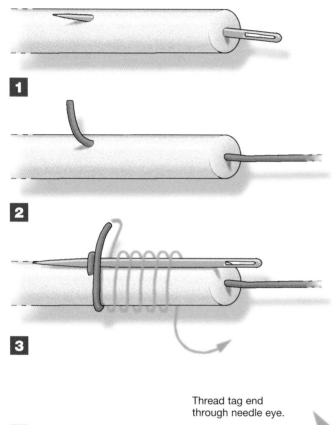

1

2

3

4

Thread tag end through needle eye.

Pull needle and tag end through.

Function

This modified nail knot makes a strong attachment for a mono leader to a fly line.

Tying

Push a needle into the end of the fly line, at a slight angle, so that it comes out again through the side. Then push the working end of the mono through the hole that has been made (*figures 1–2*). Slice the end of the mono leader obliquely for an easier passage. If the hole tends to shrink and obstruct passage of the leader's end, try heating the needle (gently) and—taking care to protect the hand —make the hole. Begin a series of wrapping turns with the mono, around the fly line, enclosing the needle (*figures 3–4*), and then pull the end through beneath the turns with the needle. Tighten and trim (*figure 5*).

5

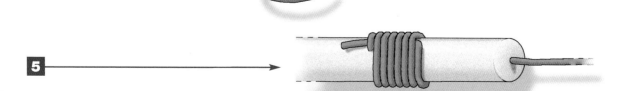

Needle knot loop

(or mono loop)

Function

Use this contrivance to facilitate frequent changes of leader and fly line.

Tying

Pass the two ends of a mono loop through a pre-made hole in the fly line—see the needle knot on the previous page for how to do this—then wrap both working ends together and tuck them to tie the knot (*figure 1*). Tighten and trim (*figure 2*).

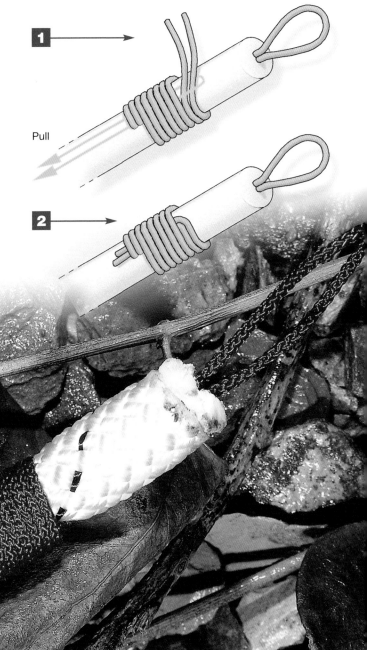

Blood loop dropper knot
(tied in the standing part)

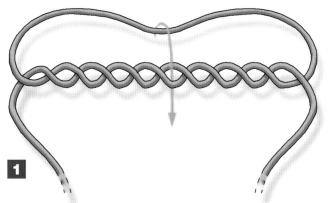

Function
Standing out at right angles to the fishing line, blood loop droppers are for attaching extra flies (droppers) or additional sea fishing hooks and sinkers (weights) in a paternoster system.

Tying
Tie a multiple overhand knot in the standing part of the line and locate the central space or compartment (*figure 1*). Then simply pull the large loop or mouth of the knot down through it (*figure 2*). Partially tighten the knot until it flypes into a blood knot form, then fully tighten it (*figure 3*).

1

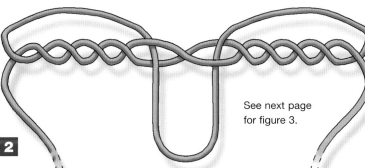

2

See next page for figure 3.

Reverse of knot; see next page for the front of the knot.

Blood loop dropper knot

(tied in the standing part, *continued*)

3

Blood loop dropper knot
(tied in the ends)

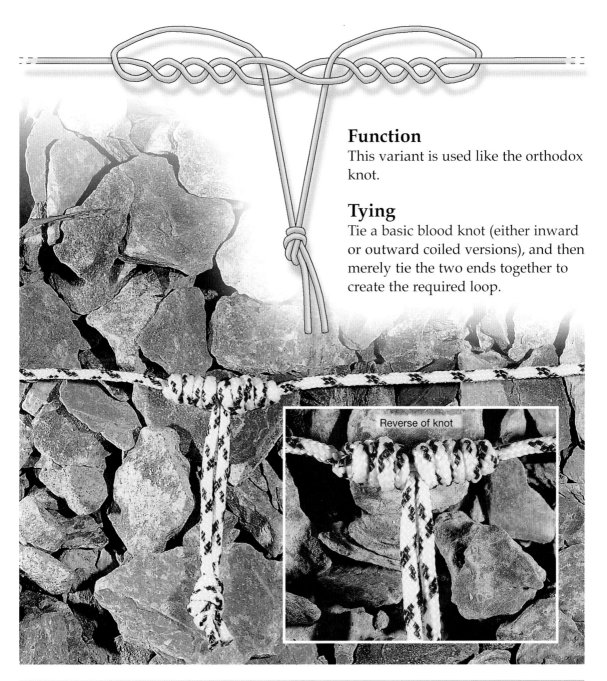

Function

This variant is used like the orthodox knot.

Tying

Tie a basic blood knot (either inward or outward coiled versions), and then merely tie the two ends together to create the required loop.

Reverse of knot

Alpine butterfly loop

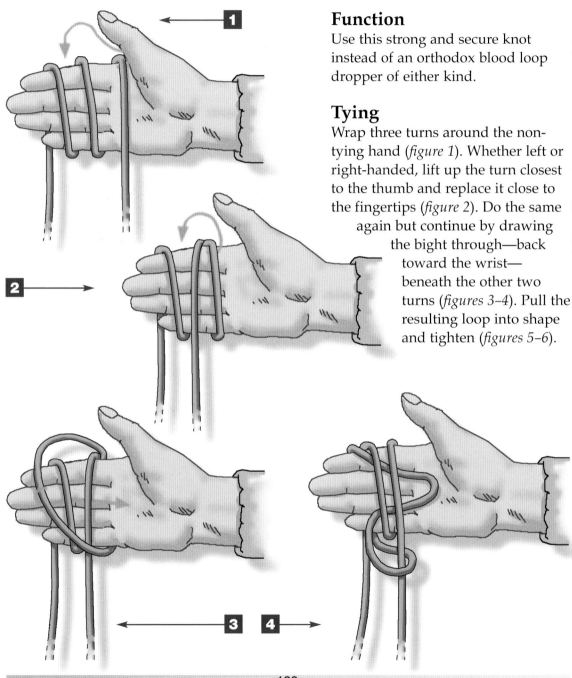

Function

Use this strong and secure knot instead of an orthodox blood loop dropper of either kind.

Tying

Wrap three turns around the non-tying hand (*figure 1*). Whether left or right-handed, lift up the turn closest to the thumb and replace it close to the fingertips (*figure 2*). Do the same again but continue by drawing the bight through—back toward the wrist—beneath the other two turns (*figures 3–4*). Pull the resulting loop into shape and tighten (*figures 5–6*).

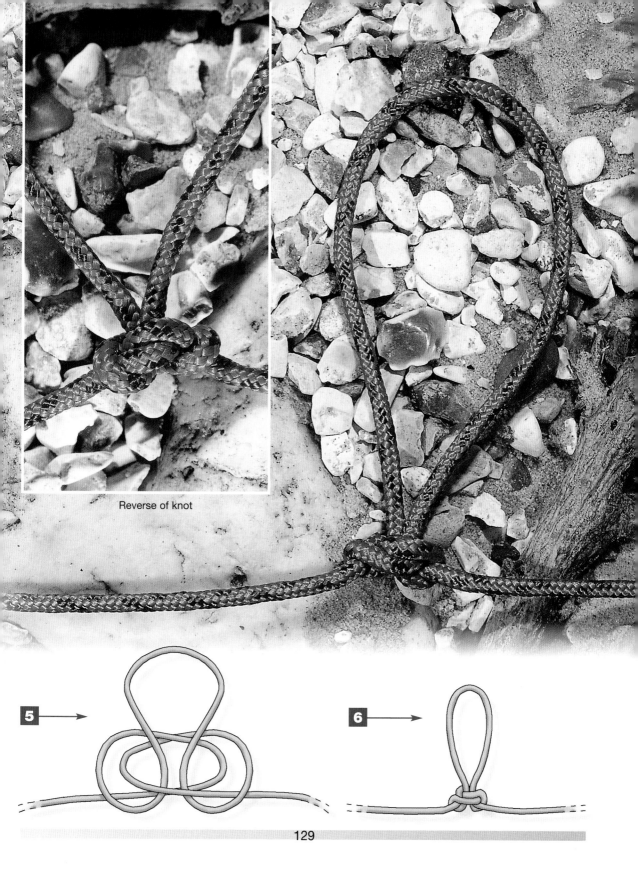

Reverse of knot

5

6

Linfit loop

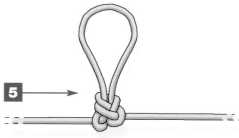

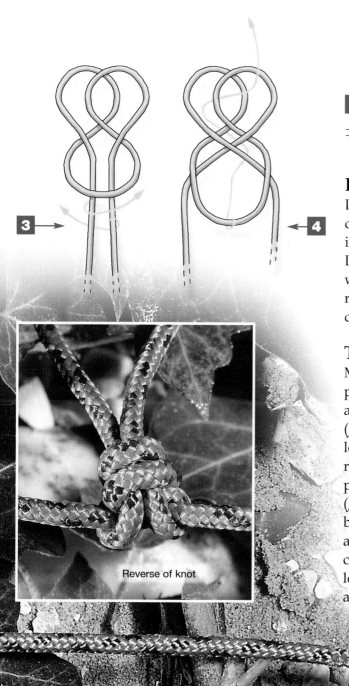

Reverse of knot

Function

Like the linfit knot, this is another comparatively new fishing knot, invented by Owen K. Nuttall of Linthwaite, Huddersfield, England, which he published in 1986 as a robust alternative to both blood loop dropper and Alpine butterfly knots.

Tying

Make a large bight in the standing part of the line, bending it forward and down to form twin loops (*figure 1*). Impart a half-twist to each loop (left-hand counter-clockwise, right-hand clockwise) and then partially cross right over left (*figures 2–3*). Pull the lower loop up behind all of the knot parts and make a final locking tuck through the compartment common to both upper loops (*figure 4*). Pull the knot snug and tight (*figure 5*).

SECTION 5

Mavericks and Mutations

"Frustrating as they can be, it is impossible to get along without knots . . . one truly needs a good repertoire of knots."

(Jerry Gibbs, fishing editor—*Outdoor Life*, 1993)

Fishing at dawn

Berkley braid knot

Function

This knot was promoted by the Berkley Tackle Company to tie their so-called super braids to hooks, flies, or lures. The knot is reported to lose only 10% of the line's breaking strength. In other words, it is 90% efficient.

Tying

Double the end of the line and pass the end of the bight through the eye of the hook or other bit of tackle (*figure 1*). Bring it back alongside its two legs, then wrap a series of turns in the direction of the hook before tucking the working end of the bight through itself (*figure 2*). Tighten with care and trim to create two tag ends (*figure 3*).

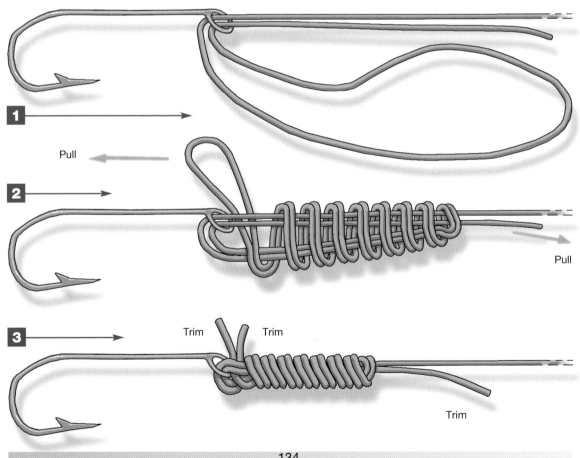

1

Pull

2

Pull

3 Trim Trim

Trim

Cat's paw

(also known as the offshore swivel knot)

Function

Used primarily for offshore big game fishing—hence its other name—this tough old ring hitch attaches long loops, such as the Bimini twist, to hooks and swivels. Should one loop or leg of the knot break, the other may hold.

1

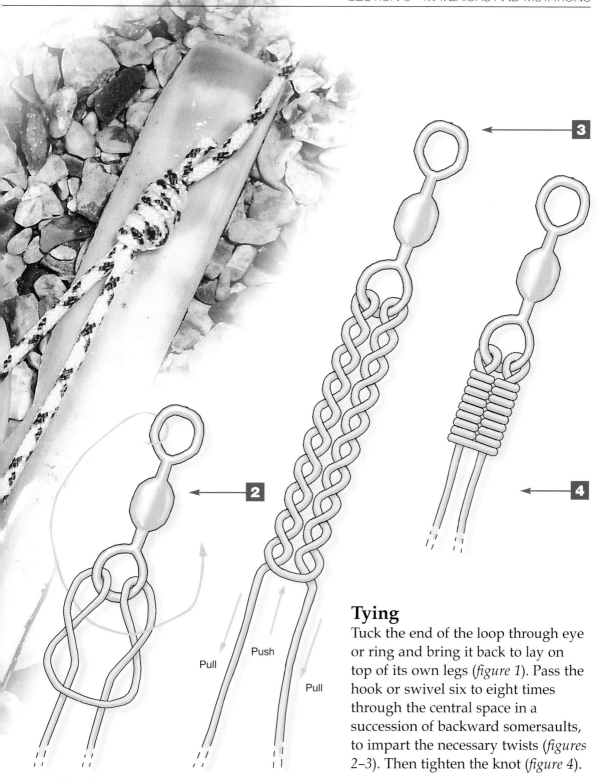

3

2

Pull   Push

Pull

Pull

4

Tying

Tuck the end of the loop through eye or ring and bring it back to lay on top of its own legs (*figure 1*). Pass the hook or swivel six to eight times through the central space in a succession of backward somersaults, to impart the necessary twists (*figures 2–3*). Then tighten the knot (*figure 4*).

Haywire twist

Function

Not strictly speaking a knot, this technique is indispensable for making a loop in single strand wire or for attaching it to hook or swivel.

Tying

Pass the working end through the eye or ring and make a loop, then impart a half-twist to create a couple of elbows (*figures 1–2*). Add at least three or four more twists, ensuring that both standing part and working end are equally involved; one must not be straight, with the other merely spiraling around it. Then bend the end of the wire at a right-angle to its standing part and begin a series of close, tight wrapping turns (*figures 3–6*). Finally, crank the end in circles until it snaps off (*figures 7–8*).

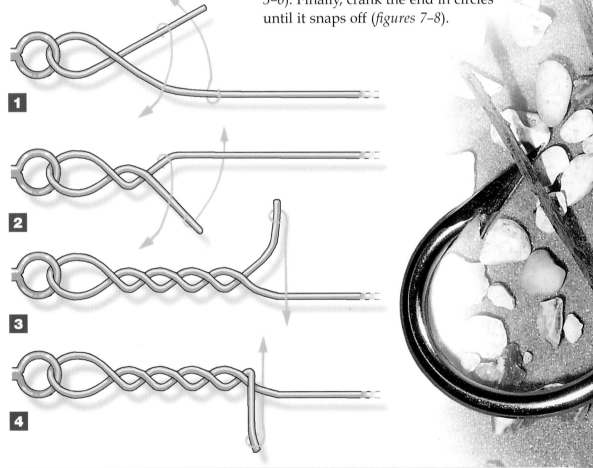

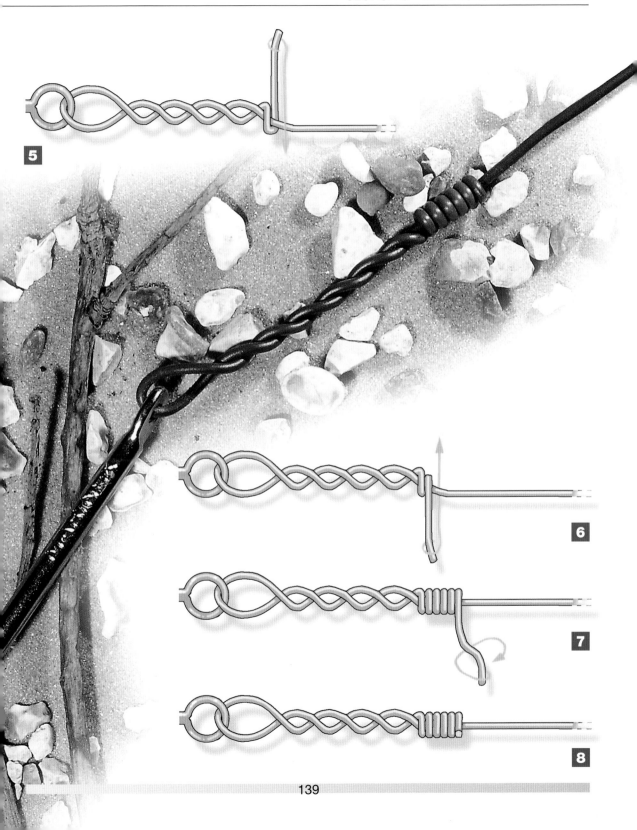

5

6

7

8

Big game loop

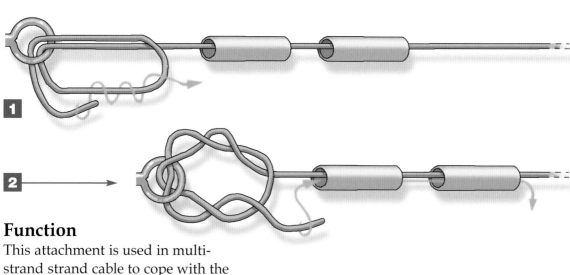

Function

This attachment is used in multi-strand strand cable to cope with the immense strains imposed by hooking marlin, huge sharks, and such.

Tying

Pass the working end of the cable through a pair of sleeves of the correct internal diameter, then tuck the end through the hook's eye to make a loop (*figure 1*). Tuck the end a second time through the eye, then wrap it repeatedly around itself (*figure 2*) before passing the end back through both sleeves once more. Neatly crimp them with the appropriate tool (*figure 3*).

Torus knot

(occasionally referred to as the Policansky knot)

Function

"Torus" is the technical name for a ring doughnut shape, and the torus knot is another reinforced loop for big game hooks and swivels.

Tying

Pass the working end through the ring or eye and make a loop. Bend the end back on itself and begin a painstaking series of tight wrapping turns (*figures 1–2*). Finally, tuck the end through the small loop at the start of the turns, and ensure that this locking turn is snug and tight (*figures 3–4*).

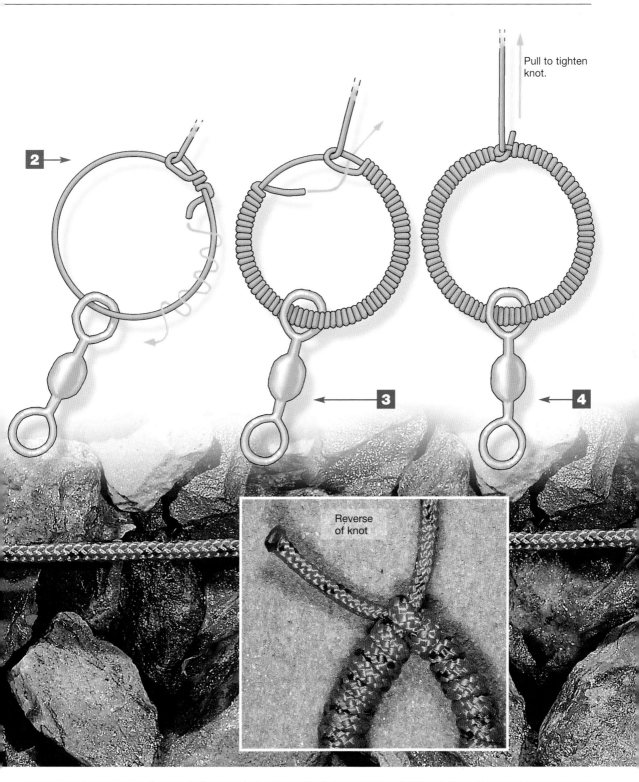

Pull to tighten knot.

Reverse of knot

Improved blood knot

Function

For joining lines of greatly different diameters, this modification of a standard knot may be the best solution.

Tying

Double the thinner of the two lines to form a long bight before laying both lines together, parallel, and pointing in opposite directions. Tie a blood knot (either outward coil, as illustrated, or inward if preferred), using the thinner line double throughout (*figure 1*). Tighten and trim (*figure 2*).

Reverse of knot

1 →

Pull

Pull

2 →

Trim

Trim

Reverse of knot

Mono to braid knot

Function

To join lines of greatly different constructions, such as mono to a super-braid loop, this is an effective knot.

Tying

Bring the two lines together, parallel, ends pointing in opposite directions (*figure 1*). Wrap the loop three times around the standing part of the lure line (*figure 2*). Then wrap the working end of the lure line five or six time around both legs of the loop, and pass it back through the end of the loop (*figure 3*). Hold the loop and pull steadily on both working end and standing part of the lure line to tighten the knot (*figure 4*).

1 →

Mono tag end   Mono to lure

Braided line

2 →

3 →

Pull

Pull

Mono to lure

4 →

Trim

Leader to wire leader knot

Function

Add a short length
of wire to a leader with
this knot when it is necessary
to combat the cutting power of a
fish's teeth.

Tying

Make a bight in the wire. Introduce
the mono or braid leader and create a
series of wrapping turns, working
away from the end of the bight.
Bring the end back and tuck it
through beside its own standing part
(*figure 1*). Tighten and trim (*figure 2*).

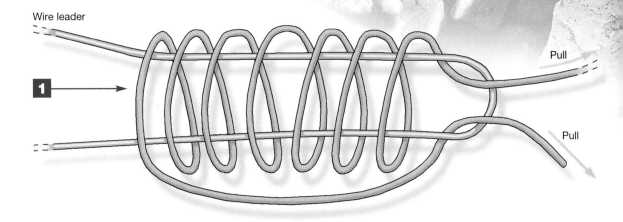

Wire leader

1

Pull

Pull

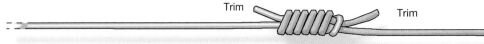

Trim

Trim

2

Huffnagle knot

Function

This must be the most inelegant of all angling knots. It was developed in South Florida to join a light fly leader tippet to very heavy mono of 80–120 lbs (36–54 kgs).

Reverse of knot

Tying

Tie a long loop, such as a Bimini twist, in the lighter line before joining the two together with a fisherman's knot—a grinner tied with a pair of single overhand knots (*figure 1*)—in such a way that a length of the mono bight is left. Wrap this three times around the thicker line and flype it to form a half-blood knot (*figure 2*). Tug everything tight and trim four tag ends (*figure 3*).

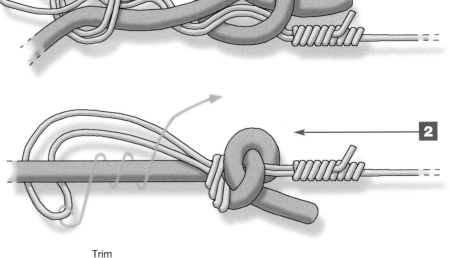

Trim

Trim

Trim

Ligature knot

(twined and twisted)

Function

Use this knot for joining lines of identical size that may slip in less elaborate knots. The number of twists and tucks will vary with the size of the lines being tied—less for thicker ones, more for thinner.

Tying

Cross both working ends, left over right, and tie a triple half-knot (*figures 1, 2, 3*). Cross the ends, again left over right, and tie an identical triple half-knot (*figures 4–5*). Pull steadily on both ends and standing parts, tightening the knot, and at the same time encouraging it to twist into its final form (*figures 6–7*).

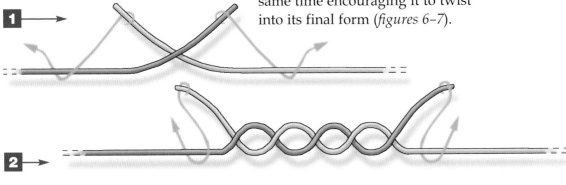

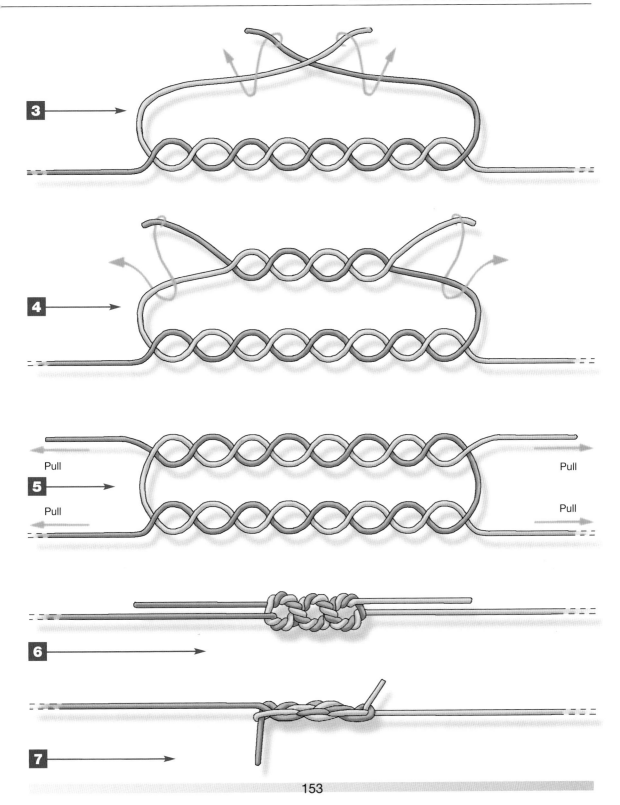

3

4

5 Pull

Pull

Pull

Pull

6

7

Tandem hook knot

Function

Adding a second hook below the first requires a simple but secure intermediate knot such as this.

Tying

Pass the working end of the mono or braid through the eye of what will be the upper one of the two hooks and tie a double overhand knot—in effect, a minimal nail knot—around the shank (*figure 1*). Tighten this knot close to the eye, then add a second hook at the end of the line (*figure 2*).

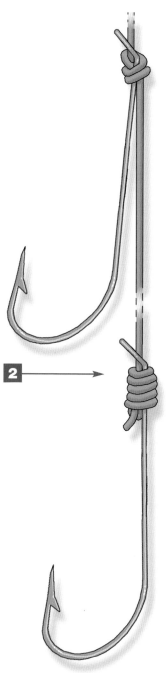

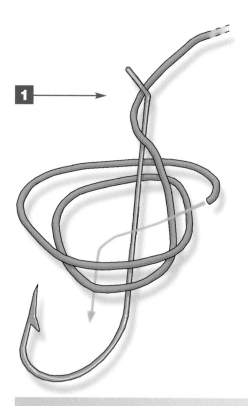

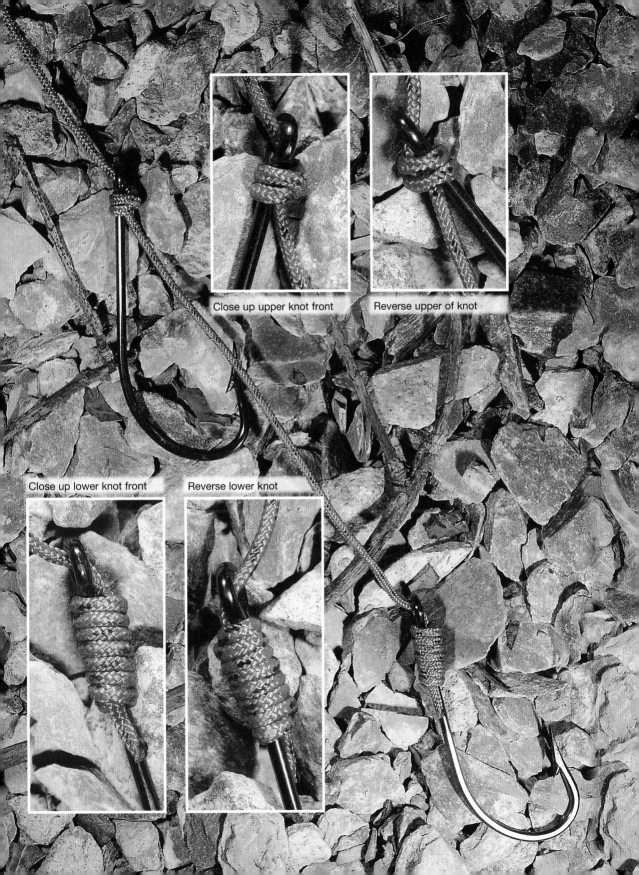

Close up upper knot front

Reverse upper of knot

Close up lower knot front

Reverse lower knot

Knotless knot

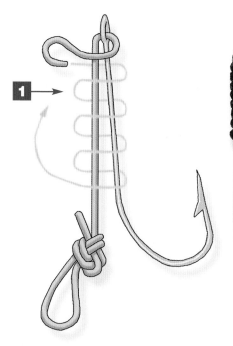

1

2

3

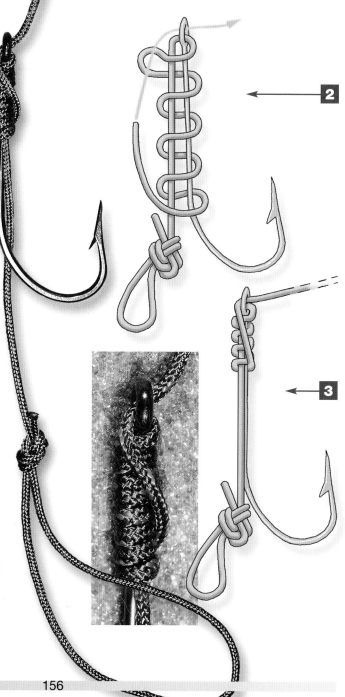

Function

There are alternative approaches to the tandem hook knot, which leave the end of the line free for adding another hook or other item of tackle hardware, and this is one.

Tying

Lead the working end up alongside the shank of the hook and pass it through the eye (*figure 1*). Make a series of tight wrapping turns down around the shank, enclosing the standing part of the line, then bring the end back to tuck once more through the hook's eye (*figures 2–3*). Tighten.

Arbor	The spindle at the middle of a reel or spool to which fishing line is attached.
Backing line	Monofilament or braid loaded onto a fly reel before the fly line, to which it is joined, to add bulk to the reel and cope with long runs.
Bight	A partial loop in the form of a U-shape.
Blood knot	The collective name for a family of strong and secure knots, comprised of numerous wrapping turns, that are particularly suited to use in fishing lines.
Braid	Plaited or interwoven line, generally polyester (trade names: Dacron, Terylene), that is stronger and more durable than nylon monofilament.
Breaking strength	The load that manufacturers calculate will cause a line to part, under optimum conditions, taking no account of wear, knots, or other weakening factors.
Butt	The thicker part of the mono leader attached to the fly line.
Elbow	Two crossing points, close together, created by a twisted bight.
Eye	A small loop in line.
Fly line	An attachment between fly and leader of coated nylon, Dacron, or PVC.
Flype	(rhymes with "type") An archaic Scottish dialect word, still current in tying knots, meaning to turn inside out by a peeling process.
Knot	The generic word for all deliberate (and accidental) tucks and tangles, including those that join lines together, create fixed loops and sliding nooses, or attach lines to hooks, lures, swivels, and sinkers.
Lead	(pronounced "leed") The direction taken by the working end of a line as it forms a knot.
Leader	A short length of nylon monofilament, Dacron braid, or wire attaching a hook, fly or other lure to a fly line.
Line	A general word for any kind of monofilament, braid, or wire used as part of a tackle assembly.
Loop	A bight that has acquired a crossing point.
Loop knot	A fixed loop, as opposed to a noose.
Lure	An artificial bait.
Monofilament (mono)	Nylon fishing line.
Nip	The location(s) within a knot where friction is concentrated.

Noose	A sliding, adjustable loop knot.
Nylon	A synthetic material widely available in two grades: nylon 66 and nylon 6.
Plug	An artificial bait, resembling an animated fish, that conceals a hook.
Polyester	A synthetic material (trade names: Dacron, Terylene).
Security	The property of a knot to withstand shock loading and intermittent jerks without slipping or coming apart.
Snelling	The collective term for knotting a line to the shank of a hook, designed especially for spade-ended or eyeless hooks.
Standing end	The inactive, unused end of a line.
Standing part	Any unemployed section of line between standing and working ends.
Strength	The ability of a knot to withstand a load without breaking
Super lines	Remarkably strong braided lines, made from the latest man-made materials with exceptional strength-to-weight ratios.
Swivel	An item of tackle hardware designed to prevent twists in the line.
Tag (or tag end)	the knotted end of a line, particularly when that end has been trimmed off close to the knot.
Tippet	The thin terminal section of the leader, to which the fly is attached.
Working end	the end of a line actively involved in tying a knot.

The following books devoted exclusively to fishing knots and rigs are in order of date of publication (most recent first). Older ones may only be obtainable from second-hand book dealers.

Guide to Rigging Braid, Dacron and Gelspun Lines, Geoff Wilson, (Australia 1999) Australian Fishing Network

The Hamlyn Book of Fishing Knots, Geoffrey Budworth, (UK 1999) Octopus Publishing Group Ltd

Fly Leaders & Knots, Larry V. Notley, (USA 1998) Frank Amato Publications, Inc.

The Pocket Guide to Fishing Knots, Peter Owen, (USA 1998) Burford Books, (UK 1998) Merlin Unwin Books

The Little Red Fishing Knot Book, Harry Nilsson, (Canada 1997) self-published:

Complete Book of Fishing Knots & Rigs, Geoff Wilson, (Australia 1995) Australian Fishing Network

Fishermen's Knots, Fishing Rigs, and How to Use Them, Bob McNally, (USA 1993) McNally Outdoor Publications

Practical Fishing Knots, Mark Sosin and Lefty Kreh, (UK 1991) B.T. Batsford Ltd

The Hardy Book of Fisherman's Knots, Alan B. Vare, (UK 1987) Camden Publishing Co. Ltd

Fisherman's Knots and Nets, Raoul Graumont & Elmer Wenstrom, (USA 1948) Cornell Maritime Press

Anglers' Knots in Gut and Nylon, Stanley Barnes, (Birmingham, England 1948) Cornish Brothers Limited

Fisherman's Knots & Wrinkles, W.A. Hunter, (London, England 1927) A. & C. Black Limited

Fishing-knot books may also be found and purchased via the Internet. Simply search for "angling knots."